THE ORIGINS OF HUMANKIND

Stephen Tomkins
Director of Studies for Biological Sciences
Homerton College, Cambridge

SECOND EDITION

CAMBRIDGE
UNIVERSITY PRESS

PUBLISHED BY THE PRESS SYNDICATE OF THE UNIVERSITY OF CAMBRIDGE
The Pitt Building, Trumpington Street, Cambridge CB2 1RP, United Kingdom

CAMBRIDGE UNIVERSITY PRESS
The Edinburgh Building, Cambridge CB2 2RU, United Kingdom
40 West 20th Street, New York, NY 10011-4211, USA
10 Stamford Road, Oakleigh, Melbourne 3166, Australia

First published 1984
Second edition published 1998

Designed and typeset in Palatino 9.5pt by Hart McLeod, Cambridge

Printed in the United Kingdom at the University Press, Cambridge

A catalogue record for this book is available from the British Library

ISBN 0 521 46676 8 paperback

Cover design by Chris McLeod

Cover photo: *Homo habilis* specimen KNM–ER 1813
(Natural History Museum, London)

The publisher would like to thank the following for permission to reproduce diagrams and
photographs:
Punch (Figure 1.1); Steve Jones, Robert Martin and David Pilbeam [Cambridge University
Press] (Figures 5.3, 5.4, 5.5 and 9.5); John Reader/Science Photo Library (Figure 7.7); Alan
Hughes, by permission of Professor P. V. Tobias (Figure 8.1); John Rodford/Don
Johanson/Granada (Figure 8.2); Natural History Museum, London (Figure 9.7); Z. Burian
(Figure 10.1); Alan Walker/National Museums of Kenya (Figure 10.3); P. E. Ross/*Scientific
American*, courtesy of L. L. Cavalli-Sforza (Figure 11.7); French Tourist Office (Figure 11.8);
Duncan Brown (Figure 12.3); British Museum (Figure 12.5).

Contents

Contents

Preface

We have undergone a revolution in our understanding of the human story in the century and a half since Darwin wrote his most important book, the *Origin of Species*. Just a century ago the impact of the idea of our descent from the anthropoid apes was cushioned by the sheer lack of fossil evidence for it. Throughout the twentieth century missing pieces of the great jigsaw puzzle have fallen into place. There are now so few missing links in the chain that runs from the ancestor we have in common with the chimpanzee that an anti-evolutionist has little grounds for opposition to the idea. What is so exciting is that all the absent pieces of the jigsaw puzzle certainly exist, in places like the Great Rift Valley of Africa, still waiting to be discovered. However, a knowledge of fossil patterns by no means answers all the important questions in this human story. Darwin unveiled the mechanism of natural selection. We are still only beginning to understand the complexity of the genetic processes that occur in evolution. Each of us in our own development is a re-enactment of a developmental drama that has been played out successfully in every generation since life began. Each of us has genetic contributions from a host of antecedents. Every one of us also has some genetic novelty that has never existed before, either by virtue of recombination or by virtue of new mutations. All our ancestors survived to reproduce themselves successfully, but that is not a foregone conclusion for each of us. The first upright apes that walked the wooded savannahs of Africa, 4 million years ago, were not as intelligent as ourselves; they were not human. But now we know enough about them to see how they might have changed, developing a culture that steadily built up in support of their increasingly complex biological nature. These times were long before the relatively recent events of the Neolithic revolution and the development of the earliest human civilisations. Prehistory ends where written history begins.

Students reading this book need to know how it is designed for their use. It starts by setting the scene historically. Evolution is a key idea and you need to re-live Darwin's developing perception of it. Chapters 2 to 6 will help you understand the processes of evolution. The story that follows in chapters 7 to 12 takes the human journey progressively through time. Each chapter could be read at a single sitting, and ends with a few 'questions to think about' that are designed to help you think for yourself about the material and some of the issues raised. If you are working towards an examination, make sure that the focus of your study is guided by the examination syllabus. Make collections of drawings of appropriate fossil evidences and of the human family trees. Do not become disheartened by such matters as the complexity of names and dates; gradually your understanding will increase. Do not treat the human saga as a 'just so' story. The study of fossil humans is an experimental science in the sense that hypotheses are continually constructed and predictions made on the basis of observations and evidence. Try to enter imaginatively into the construction of 'scenarios', but, equally, demand that the evidence be convincing to a sceptically minded person. When you have read this book and thought about human origins you may not see yourself in quite the same way again!

Author's acknowledgements

I should like to pay tribute to those whose help, encouragement, inspiration or advice were formative in the first edition of this book, including Alan Cornwell, Edward Holden, Don Johanson, Joseph Hutchinson, Maeve Leakey, Thurstan Shaw, David Pilbeam, Chris Stringer and Alan Walker. Along the way I have been helped by discussions with innumerable students and colleagues. Years ago Alan Walker showed me the wonder and discipline of digging for bones. Michael Reiss and Jonathan Kingdon have been wise and inspirational friends; I owe much to Jonathan for his infectious passion for all that has come out of Africa.

I would like to thank the series editor Alan Cornwell, Ninette Premdass and Diane Abbott of Cambridge University Press and Mitch Fitton for their infinite patience. I thank John Rodford once again for his line drawings and CUP for the use of illustrations from their excellent *Encyclopedia of Human Evolution*. More particularly, for this edition, I am grateful to Kate Robson-Brown of the Department of Biological Anthropology in the University of Cambridge, for her patient provision of references, incisive comments and guidance. Any imperfections are of my making. Lastly, I thank my wife, Helga, for putting up with another book.

ONE

The discovery of evolution

Nothing in Biology makes sense except in the light of Evolution.

Theodosius Dobzhansky (1900–75)

1.1   Human origins

The picture we have today of human origins is one of slow change in form and character over a very long period. Such a transformation is what we mean by the word **evolution**. We now live happily with this idea, but it is historically quite new and not all the implications have yet penetrated the thinking of most people. On the full evolutionary time-scale of millions of years the origins of agriculture and civilisation just a few thousand years ago are like yesterday in a vastly longer and very different human story.

How should we begin to explore this idea of human evolution? Since you were an infant, what you have learned about human origins, at school or from stories in books, film and television, has provided you with the cultural context for your own world picture. You believe that life evolved long ago, that dinosaurs existed and became extinct. You believe that there were cave-men. You might even believe (mistakenly) that the Flintstone family lived at the same time as the dinosaurs. In other words, you probably take evolution for granted.

We ought to recognise that this notion of change is not shared by everyone. Indeed, you might not have been brought up in such a culture, where evolution is a part of the picture: one cannot, after all, see evidence for things evolving in everyday life – one species is not visibly changing into another. You might have been reared within a non-evolutionary, or even hostile anti-evolutionary, world view. Many millions of people have a totally different outlook to yourself. All the traditional societies of the modern world which have been studied have in their folklore a distinct and clearly told creation story. Pre-Christian Britain had powerful Celtic myths of gods such as Dagda the Protector and Danu the Earth Mother. In part, these stories existed to answer Celtic children's questions as to where the first man and woman came from but they also served, structurally, to give young people a meaningful social context. They are not, in this sense, stories that were 'wrong'.

The world's **creation stories** are as varied as they are intriguing. There is often an element of divinity in the human origin; God is part of the picture. The Judaeo-Christian Bible story of Adam and Eve, historically shared by Jews, Muslims and Christians, is the prevailing cultural creation myth of our Western society. Adam is made from the dust of the Earth and Eve from one of his ribs. In Greek myths humans came from fish. In Hindu myths the prevalence of monkey-gods gives a different insight. The creation myth sets the cultural context for human distinctiveness. We learn of Adam and Eve's 'fall' – a formulated expression of that human characteristic of self-awareness which largely marks humans out as distinct from other animals. Biblical 'truth' can be meaningful and should not be dogmatically dismissed simply because it does not fit comfortably into a scientific way of thinking.

It would be to misjudge contemporary so-called 'primitive people', or our ancestors of a few hundred years ago, if we considered them stupid for not having our modern perception of evolution. The aboriginal human mind was certainly different from our own but just as intelligent. If you consider yourself a reasonable and thoughtful person it serves no useful purpose to condemn as 'false' other cultural ideas that have not been developed in your own society. Children genuinely need stories about human origins and these stories, learned at our parent's knee or at Sunday school, will often have a moral attached. We need not confuse science's disciplined way of thinking with the quite separate insights of religion into human nature. There are innumerable scientists who find that their understanding of human nature, as seen through evolution, is fully mirrored and supported in the human insights of both ancient literature and contemporary religious study. There are also many scientists who see no need for religion. There are even more completely unscientific people who see no point in thinking about evolution at all.

1.2   Early scientific ideas excluded evolution

The early beliefs of Western culture were based upon the creation insights of the biblical Jewish story and the classical writings of the Greeks. These cultural roots were brought together during the fifteenth century in a rebirth of learning known as the Renaissance. Nobody had seen one species turn into another, so the concept of evolution was simply unnecessary. The Christian idea of a creator God who set things in motion with a purpose was combined with the discipline of Greek logical thinking: it was argued that if God had made things to work, then the mechanisms of nature could be observed and imitated in technology. Throughout the Renaissance scientists like Leonardo da Vinci and Vesalius carried out investigations of human anatomy and natural history and laid the foundations for a clearer understanding of the affinity between humans and apes; but still there was no thought of evolution. A big upset did begin when the astronomers Copernicus and, later, Galileo asserted that the Earth moved around the Sun. This **Copernican revolution** upset the dominant authority of the Church in matters scientific, and began a revolution in thinking about science that is still with us today. From the fifteenth century ocean navigation and global exploration became much more possible. This too enlarged human knowledge of both science and nature, but nothing challenged the biblical creation story until the eighteenth century.

1.3   Carl von Linné (1707–78)

In Sweden, in the mid-eighteenth century, **Carl von Linné** (commonly latinised as 'Linnaeus') developed a hierarchical classification system for describing the great variety of plants and animals that were daily arriving in Europe because of the extensive global explorations of the time. It was essential to produce some classificatory order out of this chaos of new information. In his **Systema Natura**, published between 1736 and 1758, von Linné grouped organisms according to their physical similarity. Logically, humans were grouped with the other man-like (anthropoid) apes as a primate, the first and foremost ranking of mammals. As the chimpanzee is a creature with clear human similarities, it was originally given the name *Pan satyrus*, after a mythic semi-bestial woodland god. Quite certainly von Linné did not intend his tree-like system of classification to be taken as an evolutionary picture.

1.4   Jean Baptiste Lamarck (1744–1829)

The Linnaean system was so much more practical than anything that had preceded it that it was soon in use throughout Europe. In pre-Revolution France, a group of distinguished natural scientists led by Georges Leclerc, the Comte de Buffon, adopted this system of classification, but de Buffon now saw in it a possible blueprint for change in related forms. De Buffon, who kept the Royal Botanic Garden in Paris, clearly thought that at least some species were able to change. His pupil and successor at the 'Jardin du Roi' was **Jean Baptiste Lamarck**. Lamarck not only proposed that the diversity of plants and animals might be explained by evolution, but also propounded the first theories to account for such a view of nature. Although he survived the French Revolution and went on to write extensively about animal biology, Lamarck died unrecognised for his science, ridiculed and in poverty.

1.5   Charles Darwin (1809–82)

Charles Darwin's name is synonymous with the word 'evolution', but he was not the architect of the idea – either in England or even, as it happens, in his own family. There was plenty of radical thought in England at the time of the French Revolution. People were questioning long-held assumptions. It is interesting that Darwin's grandfather, the English physician, philosopher and naturalist **Erasmus Darwin**, wrote a poem in 1796 which toyed with the idea of evolutionary change and which actually pre-dated Lamarck's work. Charles Darwin never met his philosophical grandfather, who died in 1802 before Charles was born. **Charles Darwin** deserves the most important place in the history of biology and of evolutionary thought because of his astonishing amassing of evidence and his extensive writing and sifting of ideas. Eventually he also gathered the courage to propound ideas on evolution and, significantly, he came up with a much more plausible mechanism to explain evolution than his evolutionist predecessor Lamarck. Within a few years of his publication of the *Origin of Species*, in 1859, those who followed his views were already calling themselves 'Darwinians'. Today we use the term **Darwinism** to describe his original theory.

Charles Darwin's life is well documented. There are several excellent biographies which students should read. The most exciting tales are to be found in his *Voyage of the Beagle*, the diary of his round-the-world trip made between 1832 and 1836.

Darwin enjoyed an excellent boyhood training in the ways of wildlife, spending much time riding, fishing and shooting. As a Cambridge University divinity student, the young Charles Darwin was trained by his Professor as a systematic Linnaean. However, he didn't do much academic work at university, showing no aptitude for medicine or theology. On leaving university with a rather poor degree, he leapt at the chance to be a gentleman companion to the captain of a naval ship, the *Beagle*, carrying out survey work on the coasts of South America. **The *Beagle* Journal** shows that, by the age of 24, the young Darwin was convinced that species, as witnessed by the fossil record, might be transformed over time and that living species were altered by divergent adaptation on the different islands and continents that he visited.

On his return, Darwin had a rich collection of specimens and stories to work from, and he set about developing his reputation as a professional scientist. In 1837, a year after his return, he began his evolution notebooks in which he slowly accrued the extensive evidence for what he now felt was a theory that would change the whole perception of the natural world. He wrote subsequently … 'I occasionally sounded out not a few naturalists, and never came across a single one who seemed to doubt the permanence of species.' Darwin had trained in biblical theology and it made him sick to think of the historical and human implications of his theory. In his mind the gap between humans and animals narrowed continually as he perceived the age of the Earth extending back thousands and even millions of years before biblical accounts. He had seen at first hand the diversity of animals and fossils. In Tierra del Fuego he had been shocked to meet the Fuegians: in the whole of the Americas they were the most primitive naked hunter-gatherer aboriginals. He had met degraded African slaves living in brute squalor. The evolution of humanity from ape-like ancestors, passing through a period of primitive savagery, was increasingly inescapable for him. Humans had made a very long journey. The biblical creation was clearly a myth.

1.6   Natural selection is born

Darwin was not at all at ease with his discovery of evolution, but he was immensely determined to understand the idea. The germ of the theory of **natural selection** came to him in early 1838 after reading an essay on human population by **Thomas Malthus**. This clergyman's observations on the plight of the English rural poor, who were producing more children than they had the capacity to feed, were socio-economic rather than biological. The essay would have meant much to a young, wealthy and liberal minded gentleman, who had estates and many employees to care for. Darwin wrote of his break-through:

> *I happened to read ... Malthus, on Population, and being well prepared to appreciate the struggle for existence, which from my long continued observations of the habits of animals and plants everywhere goes on, it at once struck me that under the circumstances favourable variations would tend to be preserved and unfavourable ones to be destroyed. The result of this would be the formation of new species. I had at last a theory by which to work.*
>
> Life and letters of Charles Darwin, *Darwin, F. (ed.) (1887)*

Over the following years Darwin built up his theory, gathering every evidence of the variation upon which selection might act. Nevertheless, he was plagued by self-doubt and indecision; it even made him ill. In 1844 he confided his ideas to a group of friends. On the one hand Darwin was convinced that his theory was correct, but on the other he could not bring himself to face the consequences of such a theory being publicly debated in his name. In 1858 his hand was forced. **Alfred Russel Wallace**, a fellow naturalist collector and later a famed zoogeographer, wrote to Darwin spelling out an independently derived theory that was an almost identical exposition of his own idea formulated 14 years earlier. Thus Wallace and Darwin published a joint paper at the Linnaean Society in September of that year. Neither of them appeared at the meeting; Wallace was abroad and Darwin was too sick to attend. Perhaps to Darwin's relief the paper was ignored by the scientific community. Darwin realised that a larger work was needed for there to be any informed public debate. Urged on by friends, he began his

Figure 1.1 A *Punch* cartoon first published in 1881

work on 'the transmutation of species' without further delay. After '13 months and ten days' hard labour' the ***Origin of Species*** was published in November 1859. Darwin commented … 'It is no doubt the chief work of my life.' As he had expected, Darwin was then caricatured by the popular press, appearing in several cartoons as a monkey. There were immediately great debates and discussions in the scientific press. Darwin shunned the limelight but continued extensive writing and research. By the time of his death in 1882 he had earned a place for himself 'amongst the great Englishmen' and was buried in Westminster Abbey.

1.7 Evolution in the twentieth century

The idea of evolution has gained and grown in strength. It has proved to be an idea quite as revolutionary to society as the Sun-centred view of the solar system introduced by Copernicus 400 years earlier. The importance of the **Darwinian revolution**, as we now see it, is in the numerous biological perceptions and social ideas that have fallen into place within its enormous scope. Its implications touch every biological science.

In the twentieth century, the new science of **genetics** gave Darwinism its real boost. Indeed we might call the past 100 years 'the genetic century', for Mendel's work (unknown during his own lifetime in the nineteenth century) was rediscovered in 1900 and the concept of the particulate gene was born. Soon genetic chromosomal theory became well understood, and the molecular biology of the gene was revealed by Crick and Watson in the 1950s. Mutation theory, population genetics, selection theory and the idea of the selfish gene have all followed in Darwin's wake. Huge advances in plant and animal breeding, in behaviour studies and in medicine have followed our understanding of genetic processes. Although some molecular genetic change may now be seen to be non-Darwinian (see chapter 3), the powerhouse behind evolutionary change is undoubtedly the process of selection operating on the great pool of variation provided by mutation and the sexual reassortment of genetic material.

Evolutionary theory caught hold in the free-enterprise **progressivist culture** of the late nineteenth century. For the Victorians, evolution equated with progress. Some of Darwin's contemporaries clearly feared that the ruthlessness of natural selection would undermine the perspective of a caring Christian culture. In 1860 the geologist Adam Sedgwick, reviewing the *Origin of Species*, ventured the prophecy that if Darwin's ideas were accepted humanity 'would suffer a damage that might brutalise it and sink the human race into a lower state of degradation than any to which it has fallen since records tell us of its history'. Alfred Tennyson, the Victorian poet, saw 'Nature, red in tooth and claw'. Today we might well ask whether Darwinism, with its struggle for existence and survival of the fittest, has not affected our interpretation of society and social relationships. It may be politically convenient to use Darwinism as an excuse, but a ruthless '**social Darwinism**' has been used to rationalise economic competition and even racist politics.

1.8 Is evolution a fact?

Many scientists insist that evolution is still only a theory, and not hard fact comparable to the more testable realities and phenomena of physical science. Is this fair? One should be able to show that a scientific phenomenon can be repeated and, if it is true, fail to be able to demonstrate that it is false. Although, on the large scale, evolutionary theory cannot be tested fully, one may demonstrate conclusively all the areas of evidence in genetics that underpin the theory. One may easily prove the power of selection and demonstrate that selection works just as Darwin predicted. The study of plant and animal anatomy, embryology, physiology and behaviour, and the evidence of cell and molecular biology and of ancient fossils, are all truly compelling. Biology is interpreted so much through an appreciation of the evolutionary process that most biologists cannot imagine their subject without this perspective. Look at the evidence for yourself.

Questions to think about

1 Why are some people biblical fundamentalists?

2 Is believing in evolution also a religion?

3 Is Darwinian natural selection, as applied to humans, a socially dangerous idea?

TWO

The primates: our contemporary cousins

2.1 Primate classification employing the Linnaean system

The genius of Carl von Linné was to devise a system of classification that has stood the test of time. He produced in his *Systema Natura* a classification which reflects the branching patterns of evolution. Taxonomists, whose profession it is to place living things in named groups (taxa), have been working with and improving on his system for three centuries. In the Linnaean system every species is grouped with other similar species into a single genus. Genera are grouped with those most like them into families, and families with the greatest similarity into orders. Thus, the highest and largest groupings of class, phylum and kingdom have fewer and fewer shared characteristics in common, while the smallest groupings of genus and species have the most in common. It is the individuals of one species that are genetically most closely related. What Carl von Linné saw as a divinely ordered plan of organisation, the modern biologist sees as reflective of an evolved ancestry.

This Linnaean hierarchy of taxa is as follows:

There are twenty-two orders in the class Mammalia, all of which have hair, are endothermic and feed their young on milk. Mammals occupy almost every global environment and world region. Orders range from those containing the duck-billed platypus at one extreme to whales and dolphins at the other. Perhaps the least sophisticated and most generalised of these orders is that of the shrews – the Insectivora. Close to them in terms of having generalised and not specialised features is undoubtedly the order **Primates**, to which humans, apes, monkeys and lemurs belong. Primates are largely arboreal (adapted to life in trees). Although in many of the mammalian groups the basic five-digit hand is much modified and the teeth more complex in structure, this is not so in primates. Our order is, in this unspecialised sense, 'primitive' and ancient. Some primates, particularly the smaller forest dwellers, are very conservative in their form, showing little change in the past 50 million years.

Because there are often clear natural groupings in between each of the levels of the Linnaean hierarchy, it is common for taxonomists to make subsets. The prefix 'super' means above and the prefix 'sub' means below, with 'infra' being placed below even that. This leaves open the potential for a taxonomist to employ as many as 20 or 30 hierarchical levels in the whole system. For instance, the hierarchy between order and family is further sub-divided to descend:

> ORDER
> > suborder
> > > infraorder
> > > > superfamily
> > > > > FAMILY

Figure 2.1 shows the classification of humans among the primates, whose 186 species are divided into 11 distinct families. The finer classification of the hominoid superfamily is discussed later in this book. Within the family, subfamilies are often recognised. At the species level a **binomen** (two names) like *Homo sapiens*[1] has both the genus name (*Homo*) and the species name (*sapiens*). Humans are classified, therefore, not only as eukaryote, animal, chordate, vertebrate, mammalian, eutherian forms, but also as primate, anthropoid, catarrhine, hominoid, hominid, hominines, in the genus *Homo* and species *sapiens*!

2.2   The diversity of primates

Looking at all of the living primates, our contemporary cousins, we may learn much about ourselves as animals (see figure 2.2). This will help to set the context of human evolution.

---

[1] Genus and species names should be written in italic script or underlined (if you are writing long-hand). The higher taxa names should not be underlined or italicised but if used in their latinised form should have a capital letter, e.g. anthropoids are in the Anthropoidea.

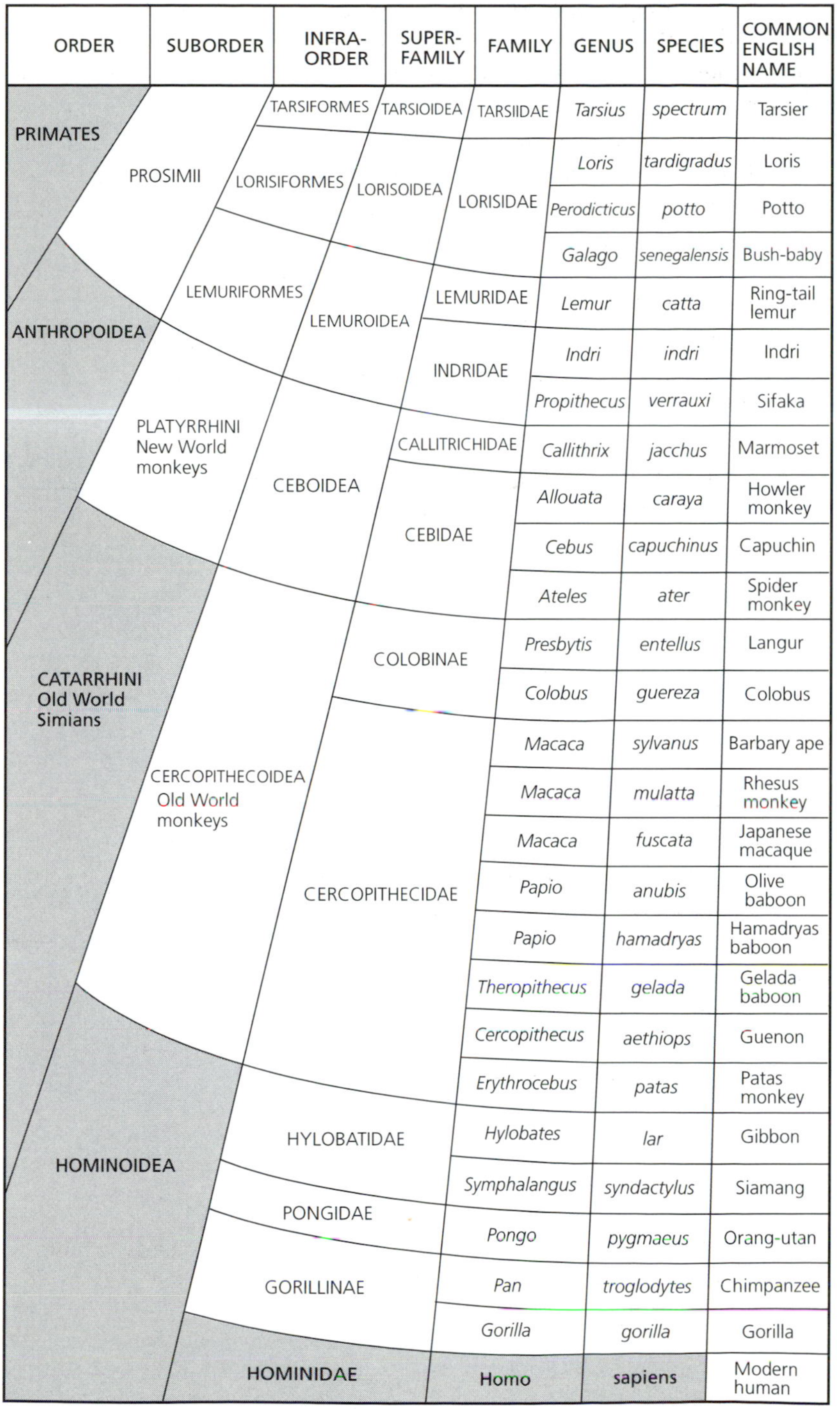

ORDER	SUBORDER	INFRA-ORDER	SUPER-FAMILY	FAMILY	GENUS	SPECIES	COMMON ENGLISH NAME
PRIMATES	PROSIMII	TARSIFORMES	TARSIOIDEA	TARSIIDAE	*Tarsius*	*spectrum*	Tarsier
		LORISIFORMES	LORISOIDEA	LORISIDAE	*Loris*	*tardigradus*	Loris
					Perodicticus	*potto*	Potto
					Galago	*senegalensis*	Bush-baby
		LEMURIFORMES	LEMUROIDEA	LEMURIDAE	*Lemur*	*catta*	Ring-tail lemur
ANTHROPOIDEA				INDRIDAE	*Indri*	*indri*	Indri
					Propithecus	*verrauxi*	Sifaka
	PLATYRRHINI New World monkeys		CEBOIDEA	CALLITRICHIDAE	*Callithrix*	*jacchus*	Marmoset
				CEBIDAE	*Allouata*	*caraya*	Howler monkey
					Cebus	*capuchinus*	Capuchin
					Ateles	*ater*	Spider monkey
	CATARRHINI Old World Simians		CERCOPITHECOIDEA Old World monkeys	COLOBINAE	*Presbytis*	*entellus*	Langur
					Colobus	*guereza*	Colobus
				CERCOPITHECIDAE	*Macaca*	*sylvanus*	Barbary ape
					Macaca	*mulatta*	Rhesus monkey
					Macaca	*fuscata*	Japanese macaque
					Papio	*anubis*	Olive baboon
					Papio	*hamadryas*	Hamadryas baboon
					Theropithecus	*gelada*	Gelada baboon
					Cercopithecus	*aethiops*	Guenon
					Erythrocebus	*patas*	Patas monkey
	HOMINOIDEA			HYLOBATIDAE	*Hylobates*	*lar*	Gibbon
					Symphalangus	*syndactylus*	Siamang
				PONGIDAE	*Pongo*	*pygmaeus*	Orang-utan
				GORILLINAE	*Pan*	*troglodytes*	Chimpanzee
					Gorilla	*gorilla*	Gorilla
				HOMINIDAE	Homo	sapiens	Modern human

Figure 2.1   The classification of humans among the primates

Figure 2.2 Representative species of primate showing the range of form and locomotor patterns in the order: (a) *Colobus*, semi-brachiation (Old World); (b) Potto, slow climbing; (c) *Ateles* (spider monkey), semi-brachiation (New World); (d) *Hylobates* (gibbon), brachiation; (e) *Microcebus* (mouse lemur), quadrupedal branch running; (f) *Pongo* (orang-utan), quadrumanous climbing; (g) *Papio* (baboon), quadrupedal walking; (h) *Gorilla*, quadrupedal knuckle walking; (i) Tarsier, vertical clinger and leaper; (j) *Homo*, bipedal walker with freed forelimbs.

Primates are divided into the anthropoids (man-like apes and monkeys) and the prosimians (literally 'before the monkeys').

Prosimians

The tarsier of Indonesia, *Tarsius*, is a useful model for an archetypal primate. The short nose, large eyes and prominent ears are striking features; the long flexible fingers have tiny pads and nail-like claws. Its teeth are well adapted for insect eating, the prey being captured by leaps from a vertical clinging position on a plant stem. For a small mammal that could nestle in your hand, it has a relatively large brain. The single young are carried clinging to their mother's fur and have great care invested in them.

The larger bush-baby of Africa, *Galago*, in the lorisid family is a similarly nocturnal vertical clinger and leaper. Although they climb hand over hand, they may leap several metres with an accuracy and co-ordination requiring sophisticated brain control. *Potto*, another forest loris, is also nocturnal but is a slow, climbing form eating fruit, tree resins and insects.

The **lemurs** are an intriguing relict family. Today they are only found on the mini-continent of Madagascar as 19 diverse species completely isolated from competition with other primates by the surrounding Indian Ocean. But fossil lemurs are known from North America and Europe and can be presumed to have been widespread but inferior competitors to the later apes and monkeys. The mouse lemur is the smallest primate known (weighing 80 g) and is exclusively nocturnal and insectivorous. Others, like the ring-tailed lemurs, are largely diurnal (day-living). These seemingly cat-like prosimians live in large social groups. Their young grow up in a troop and much time is spent in learning the skills of foraging and in grooming and other social interactions. Social group structure allows for an extended infant development time, while behavioural co-operation improves prospects for survival – as a group it is easier to evade predators and to feed efficiently.

New World monkeys

At some time in the Eocene about 50 million years ago, when the lemuroids were widespread across tropical North America and Europe, it is believed that the tectonic rifting between Greenland and Spitsbergen isolated the New World of North America from Eurasia. There is now good geological evidence for these drifting continents, and a group of North American lemuroids is believed to have given rise to the **New World monkeys**. How these ancestors of the platyrrhine ceboid monkeys (see figure 2.1) reached the then isolated continent of South America is not yet known, but it is clear that the lemurs of North America died out and the ceboids, who share with the lemurs the same primitive dental arrangement, expanded and radiated to fill all the forest niches of the great South and later Central American forests. The larger ceboids such as the spider monkey display clear parallelisms with the gibbons of Asia, but differ in having a long and prehensile tail.

Old World monkeys

The catarrhine primates (see figure 2.1) are most simply divided into the Old World monkeys, apes and humans. The sequence of events giving rise to these groups is still far from clear, but put simply, monkeys did not give rise to apes nor indeed, as we shall see, did apes as we know them today give rise to humans.

Most of the cercopithecoid **Old World monkeys** are too familiar to justify description here: the guenons of the African open woodland, the street monkeys of India and the Japanese macaques are all well known. The colobine subfamily is an exclusively herbivorous group. These are high canopy dwellers eating only leaves and fruit. Among the most interesting are the baboons and patas monkeys because they occupy a much more open environment and live away from the protection of forest trees as primitive hominids may have done. Such species in ecologically higher-risk environments, when compared to their forest counterparts, have a higher potential reproductive output and their young grow up faster and are helpless for less time.

The hominoid apes

The gibbons and great apes are far closer to ourselves. The **gibbon**'s beautiful arm-swinging locomotion through the branches of the forest is a distinctive arboreal adaptation. On the ground, out of their element, they have an intriguingly upright walking waddle. In gibbons, this brachiation (arm-swinging locomotion) and occasional bipedalism (walking on two feet) both differ in their patterns from the movement of the great apes.

The **orang-utan** is seemingly four-armed and can achieve almost any contortion up a tree. The adults are too heavy to brachiate but arm swinging

Table 2.1 The great apes

Species classification	Common name	Distribution in the wild
Pongo pygmaeus	Orang-utan	Sumatra and Borneo (Indonesia)
Gorilla gorilla gorilla	Lowland gorilla	Cameroon, Zaire
Gorilla gorilla beringei	Mountain gorilla	Uganda, Rwanda and East Zaire
Pan paniscus	Bonobo or pygmy chimpanzee	Western Zaire
Pan troglodytes	Chimpanzee	West and Central to East Africa

is very characteristic of juveniles. The two **chimpanzee** species and the largest of all apes, the **gorilla**, are too heavy as adults for a fully arboreal existence. Chimpanzees are the more arboreal, but all spend much time on the ground and walk quadrupedally on their forelimb knuckles, not on their hands as monkeys do. These **hominoids**, particularly the African **knuckle-walkers**, are closely bound up with our own evolution. The lowland and mountain gorillas, the common chimpanzee and the **bonobo** (pigmy chimpanzee) are tantalisingly like humans. Like us, they show evidence of a long arboreal adaptation (see table 2.1).

2.3   The characteristic features of primates

From the review of the diversity of the primates above, it will be seen that they are characterised by arboreal (tree-living) habits even if the larger members (including the great apes and ourselves) show more terrestrial (ground-living) behaviour.

What are the distinguishing features of primates and what is the significance of those adaptations?

1   The grasping limb
The hand is modified for grasping, there being an opposable thumb on the hand and (except in *Homo*) the foot. The hind limb is stronger and in many species shows some bipedalism. The digit claws are flattened nails. Sensitive finger-print ridges are found on all the touching hand and foot surfaces.

2   The exploratory forelimb
The radius bone of the forearm is free to rotate on its axis at the elbow, thus allowing the wrist to turn. The hand, facing up or down, feels, explores and grips objects, often bringing them up to be looked at. We take this limb mobility for granted in ourselves, but if the evolution of the primate forelimb is thought of as analogous to that of an elephant's trunk, the modification of the hand and arm in primates may be appreciated.

3   A generalised digestive system
Early primates were undoubtedly insect hunters. All primitive mammals have cutting cheek teeth with three cusps suitable for crunching up insects. Earliest primates developed a fourth cusp. Adult tarsiers have 44 sharp little teeth. The lemuroids and New World monkeys have 36 and all the adult Old World monkeys and humans have 32. All primate families have some omnivorous members and some larger forms are herbivores alone. The largest primates such as gorillas, because of their size, have the lowest metabolic energy demand per kilo of body mass and can therefore subsist on lower energy food intakes. The entirely herbivorous gorilla is well over a thousand times heavier than the entirely insectivorous mouse lemur. In primates, herbivory and size are well correlated.

4 A reduction in the sense of smell

Scent trailing is impossible through the canopy of trees and primates have little sense of smell compared to most mammals. Their reduced nose size relative to the face shortens the head. Communication by vocal sounds has seemingly replaced much communication by pheromonal scents.

5 Keen and stereoscopic vision

Leaping and accurate grasping place a premium on rapid focusing and stereoscopic vision. With an insect-hunting and nocturnal ancestry, the primates have well-developed forward-facing eyes paralleling those evolved in cats or birds of prey. Trichromatic (red/green/blue) colour cone vision is found in all diurnal primates. Both sides of the brain receive images from the two eyes, enabling accurate depth perception.

6 Large brains

Skulls of fossil primates show that, through time, their brain volumes have expanded greatly. The hindmost occipital area, concerned with visual imaging, is most enlarged. So too are the sensory areas of the cerebral hemispheres. The surface of the brain is deeply folded, providing a greater volume of surface grey matter in which information is processed. The lobes on the side of the brain associated with sound processing are enlarged. The grace and precision of a monkey moving at speed through the canopy of a forest and the athletic timing of a human gymnast are possible because of the high level of brain function.

7 Modified skulls

A more generally upright position with a forward-looking face has brought three changes in skull form. Firstly, the articulation of the head on the neck is more under its centre of gravity. The big opening (foramen magnum) through which the spinal cord emerges is further forward beneath the cranium. Secondly, reduction of the nose and muzzle shortens the face and brings the jaws more under the cranium as well. Thirdly, the eye orbits, being enlarged and forward-facing, need support in the form of a post-orbital bar, a pillar of bone behind the eye socket. Often the eye is protected with a strong bony brow-ridge.

8 Reduced number of offspring

Population biologists distinguish *r*- and *K*-strategist species. Relative to other mammals, primate species are very *K*-selected, that is they have longer-lived individuals with fewer offspring in more stable populations than the 'boom and bust' *r*-selected forms. Primates often carry a single infant and have long gestation periods, longer periods of suckling before weaning, longer infant dependency and later sexual maturation than any other comparably sized mammalian group. Infants are carried by their mothers and fed from only two mammae on the breast. Primate infants are not hurried through their childhood. The consequences of this high investment in small numbers of offspring by primates are highly significant in the human story.

9 The support of a society

Primates, especially the higher ones, lead remarkably gregarious lives. Most individuals are bonded at least loosely to mates, dependants or parents in family groups or troops. Through living in such groups, the discovery of food sources which are widely spaced but have high localised concentrations, such as fruiting trees, is easier and more efficient. Mutual defence against predators is more effective with the group's numerous ears and eyes; this corporate protection activity encourages group cohesion. Lengthy mutual grooming is highly characteristic of primates, not only serving to promote health and hygiene but also reinforcing the mutual affection and dependency of individuals. This reciprocated altruism, advanced to a high level of social interdependency, is the basis of our own human society.

2.4 Our closest animal relative: the chimpanzee

One of the most outstanding and revealing programmes of science research to be done in primate biology is that undertaken by **Jane Goodall** and her colleagues in observing the chimpanzees of the **Gombe Stream Reserve** in Tanzania. Chimps live to about 40 years. Jane Goodall has already seen a life time in the animals she has been studying in the wild. Some very old males and females in the groups were known to her as infants in the early 1960s. Due largely to Goodall's work, and the filming of these animals, millions of humans have come to see themselves mirrored in the lives of these chimps. One of Jane Goodall's early findings was that the chimpanzees use selected and fashioned twigs as tools for catching termites, by 'fishing' in the insects' burrows. Elsewhere in Africa chimps are known to use hammer stones and stone anvils for nut-cracking. It was once thought that tool use was a solely human activity. Chimps live in **territorial groups** ranging from a dozen to well over 50 individuals. They are a community of adult males and females and their offspring. Females maintain an area of family around themselves as the group moves, sometimes co-operating with one or more other adult females. Single male chimpanzees do not control or hold a group of females in any hierarchical system or territorial area. Instead the band of males within the community defends the area of that group against neighbouring group males and large carnivore predators. Mating is promiscuous with each female coming on heat (oestrous) and being mated by several males. The males seem to stay on in their home group, while young females may leave or be kidnapped by neighbouring groups. The reigning males are often closely related to each other.

There are many different social patterns in other anthropoids. Although chimps display a multi-male **polygyny** (many males with many female mates per male), the typical gorilla group, by contrast, has a uni-male polygyny with one silverback male dominating a small number of females. Orang-utans have a more dispersed arrangement like the gorilla, while gibbons, in Asia, are **monogamous**, with a strong pair-bond between a male and female. Such arrangements allow us to think not only about our physical relatedness and our differences as animals, but also about the social systems that may have evolved in chimp and ancient human society.

Questions to think about

1 Why is it easier to produce an agreed system for classifying animals and plants than it is to produce an agreed system for organising books in a library?

2 Why are you classified as a primate?

3 From what you have read or seen, what are your feelings about chimpanzee society?

THREE

Mechanisms for change

3.1 Darwin's theory of natural selection

There would not have been so much difficulty over the understanding of evolution if it had been possible simply to sit down and watch it happening. The problem was, and is, that it is just too slow a process. If, however, Darwin's theory of evolution by natural selection is carefully examined in conjunction with a knowledge of genetics there is much that can be seen to demonstrate these processes of slow change. This chapter looks at Darwin's theory in the light of what we know about genetic variation and genetic change. It is important to think of these processes as *applying to ourselves now*, for this is exactly how we may have evolved over millions of years.

Darwin's theory is most simply set down as two pairs of observations with one deduction arising from each pair (see below). The final theory itself is a further synthesis (putting together) of both deductions, and can be summarised as a diagram (figure 3.1) or as a statement. It is important in explaining Darwin's theory not to leave out any steps or its logical structure may be lost.

Observation	All known organisms produce more offspring than are required to replace them; there is **overproduction**.
Observation	The population of a species, apart from fluctuations about a mean, tends to have a fairly constant level; **populations are stable**.
Deduction	There is therefore a **struggle for existence**; many individuals perish before they can reproduce.
Observation	Organisms produce offspring which closely resemble their parents; **like produces like**.
Observation	Organisms are variable and the offspring of any two parents reproducing sexually will be varied; **like may produce unlike**.
Deduction	In any species there is **inheritable variation**.

Each of the paired observations above appears at first to contradict the other, but each pair finds a synthesis in the deduction which follows. (The logical philosopher Hegel called such apparently conflicting ideas the *thesis* and *antithesis*, which find a *synthesis* in the deduction when you put them together.) Darwin's ingenuity lay in combining the two deductions together as a **theory of natural selection**. It may be stated as follows:

> *In the struggle for existence individuals are not all alike; some will have variations that are favourable, some unfavourable. Consequently, a higher proportion of individuals with favourable variations will on average survive to reproduce; a higher proportion of individuals with unfavourable variations will die before reproducing; since variation is transmitted by heredity the effects of differential survival will accumulate in each generation. This natural selection will act constantly to improve the adaptation of the species to its environment and in the course of time may generate new species entirely.*

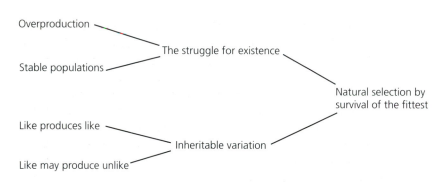

Figure 3.1   A summary of Darwin's theory of natural selection

3.2   Inheritable variation

One of the key ideas in Darwin's theory is that of **inheritable variation**. What does it mean? Let us examine the observations that have been made. When like produces like we are not really surprised; cats give birth to kittens, dogs to puppies and humans to babies. We are not surprised because we understand that each member of a species holds characteristics in common with other members of the species. Today we talk of a 'gene pool' for a species in which we see all the genetic variations able to be shared by the individuals of that species. We may recognise all sorts of variations in a species and we recognise that almost any may come together in one individual. It is useful to compare the genes to a pack of cards. Such genetic reassortment is like shuffling the pack of genes before dealing out a new hand.

However, the genetic pack of cards is not completely stable; further variation is possible. There may be new **gene mutations** resulting in the formation of altogether new genetic characters. This is an extremely rare event, but such a one in a million chance may be significant. For Darwin this was a subject of real interest. He spent much time talking to the breeders of domestic animals who had selected 'sports' (as the Victorians called them). These were oddities, from which new varieties could be produced. Darwin recognised how important human 'artificial selection' had been in domestic species. Seeing the varieties of these forms all descended from one originally wild species convinced him that a natural selection process might also pick up these novelties and bring them into the gene pool of the species.

3.3   DNA replication is not perfect

How do simple mutations arise? **DNA** replicates its organic base-pair coding faithfully, A-T, C-G, G-C and T-A. Each DNA molecule single-strand partner is the code complement of the other. When replicated to produce two identical molecules (by semi-conservative replication), the DNA molecule first unzips. Then each strand of the one parent molecule will use polymerases to acquire a new complementary strand. This is built adjacently onto the older single strand. In this way two separated new double-stranded molecules are formed, each one absolutely identical to the other. The linear code of the original molecule is identical in the new molecules. The process is near to perfection with usually 99.9999996% success. However, it is not 100% for, on average, one base pair in every 300 million base pairings is incorrect. This may be a crucial and important error.

This knowledge of mistakes in pairing comes to us from a study of the **mutation rate** of genes. A dominant mutation like achondroplasia, which produces dwarfing in people, occurs at a high frequency of 14 in every million gametes. This gene is dominant and is always expressed. We know that the mutation occurs at this rate because there are 14 in a million children with the syndrome born to normal height parents who cannot (since it is dominant) carry the faulty gene. In this condition there is a very large gene involved and there are probably many ways in which it might go wrong. It is worth considering whether a base-pair genetic change in a gene will inevitably cause harm. There are two reasons why it may not. Firstly, almost all amino acids have at least two triplet codes, so it is not inevitable that a base code change will alter the protein. Secondly, even if an amino acid is altered it may not affect the subsequent protein formation. The position and chemical nature of the residue of an amino acid is often of extreme impor-tance in secondary or tertiary structure, but there are plenty of primary structural changes that may be made that will have little effect at all. Such minor genetic changes are called **silent mutations**. They are not phenotypi-cally expressed in any change of character.

3.4   Neutral theory

In 1968 Motoo Kimura proposed a **neutral theory of evolution** at the molecular level. He suggested that most evolutionary change in molecules of protein and DNA is not a result of selection but is due to chance miscodings that may be described as **random drift**. It seems this lowest level of genetic change is dominated by random processes. Kimura and others have made extensive studies of small biomolecules and have demonstrated clearly that such changes continually go on wherever they may have a 'silent effect' which cannot be selected for or against – hence the term 'neutral'. This may contribute to the fact that many of our genes are polymorphic, having different forms at the same gene locus. Kimura's observed rates of amino acid change are slow and seem to reflect a continually shifting change in DNA coding and hence protein amino acid sequence. Neutral evolution is change at the molecular level of a non-Darwinian kind. This theory is important for understanding human evolution because some changes do appear to have a constant rate and hence may be used as a **molecular clock**, recording the passage of time between the separation of two evolutionary lines. This is examined further in sections 5.5 and 5.7.

3.5   Fitness

The theory of natural selection was soon nicknamed 'the survival of the fittest'. Fitness has precise meaning in evolutionary biology, describing the relative probability of a genotype surviving from birth to adulthood. **Darwinian fitness** should not be confused with any simple idea of physical fitness. Even if a new mutant gene has arisen by chance and is potentially of advantage to an individual, such a tiny biochemical change in DNA cannot possibly affect the course of evolution unless a number of events follow. Firstly, the gene must find 'expression'; it must operate within the genotype to affect the phenotype. Secondly, successful breeding is essential for the gene to be replicated into a larger population of individuals. Thirdly, the altered phenotype must have a higher fitness, in a Darwinian sense, than other phenotypes. Fitness is not just a question of survival but of the individual contributing more offspring to the next generation than do other individuals. The general idea of fitness is illustrated for people in Britain today by the fact that for all conceptions, 15% die in early embryonic or foetal life, 2% are still-born, neonatal deaths account for a further 1.5%, and 2% of infants fail to reach maturity. Of those that do grow to maturity, 10% remain childless, either through choice or infertility. From this example alone it can be seen how complex the process of selection may be and how many different kinds of genetic feature may be involved.

3.6   Genes in populations

Before the fitness of a single gene can be considered we may remind ourselves of how genes occur in individuals, as genes and genotypes, and how they occur in the genetic pool of a species. Most genes have a partner gene, or allele, on the corresponding homologous chromosome to the one on which they occur. These partner alleles separate in gamete formation (meiosis) and come back together again in pairs to make up the new genotype of an individual. The frequency of one particular allele in the gene pool of a species is governed by the **Hardy–Weinberg equilibrium law**. This states that the frequency of the allele will not change from generation to generation if the population is infinitely large and mating is at random. However, there are disequilibrial events that may upset stability. For example, a disproportionate selection of the possessors of that gene, either positively in its favour or negatively against it, will affect its frequency. So too will migration of possessors of the gene into or out of the population and the sampling instability that a small population brings (see section 3.9).

The story of the **peppered moth**, *Biston betularia*, and its change from the pale form to the black melanic form during a period of major industrial soot pollution in the Midlands of England is well known. It is a particularly good example of gene frequency change. The species occurs in two principal forms in England, a variety called *carbonaria* which is black and a variety called *typica* which is the usual peppered grey form, from which the moth gets its common name. The melanic *carbonaria* was first observed in 1848 near Manchester. It may have been a rare form then and not a new mutation (melanic forms of moths are often found in dark pinewood environments). Originally noted as rare by insect collectors, the black form increased in frequency dramatically. By 1900 there were less than 10% *typica* in Manchester and by 1950, just a century after its first appearance, the *carbonaria* form had increased to over 95% of the population.

Table 3.1   Relative fitness of the two forms of *Biston betularia* (peppered moth) in a polluted Birmingham woodland

	carbonaria	*typica*
Genotype	CC or Cc	cc
Phenotype	black (melanic)	grey (peppered)
Released	601	201
Recaptured	205	34
Recaptured (%)	34.1	16.9
Relative fitness	1.000	0.496

This moth was first investigated in the 1950s by Bernard Kettlewell. He realised the potential importance of this evidence in demonstrating **Darwinian selection** at work. Kettlewell guessed that the change was due to predation of the more obvious grey forms by small birds. Releasing some previously marked black and grey moths in a polluted Birmingham woodland, he only managed to recapture about half as many grey forms as might be expected from the numbers he initially released (see table 3.1). In Kettlewell's experiment it is clear that the grey moths survived less well. If the relative fitness (survival chance) of the black *carbonaria* is expressed as 1.0, that for the grey *typica* form is clearly less at about a half (0.496).

It is easy to compute from these figures the selection that would be operating in nature. Moths that are grey have approximately half as much of a chance of survival as the black forms. Using a computer program, and giving the grey moths a more generous two-thirds survival chance, one may discover the theoretical change in gene frequency in the evolution of the peppered moth (see table 3.2). There is ample time for the observed evolutionary change to occur.

It is intriguing that a reversed selection pressure is now operating in the smokeless zones of Manchester, Liverpool and Birmingham. In all these cities there are now fewer peppered moth melanics than there were at the

Table 3.2 Theoretical changes in gene frequencies in the evolution of melanism. Starting with a melanic allele (C) frequency of 0.00001 in 1848 (rounded to 0.0) and giving the peppered form a two-thirds survival rate compared to the melanics (peppered relative fitness of 0.67, i.e. selection coefficient of 0.33), the recessive peppered allele (c) becomes very rare.

Year	Generation	Gene frequency	
		C	c
1848	0	0.00	1.00
1858	10	0.00	1.00
1868	20	0.03	0.96
1878	30	0.45	0.55
1888	40	0.76	0.24
1898	50	0.86	0.14
1908	60	0.90	0.10
1918	70	0.92	0.08
1928	80	0.94	0.06
1938	90	0.96	0.04
1948	100	0.96	0.04

Source: Ridley, M., *Evolution*, Blackwell Scientific Publications 1993

height of urban pollution. Could such a gene frequency shift be found in humans? It is important to seek such evidence.

3.7 Heterozygote advantage

There may often be alleles at a gene locus that have each evolved under different selection pressures. Here, where the two different alleles rival each other in a **balanced polymorphism**, the heterozygotes may have a higher survival chance than either of the two homozygotes. The most striking example of this in humans is **sickle-cell anaemia**. In this disease a faulty haemoglobin (Hb S) replaces the normal haemoglobin (Hb A). The alleles are codominant so that heterozygotes produce both sorts of blood pigment. Sickle-cell disease in the homozygous (Hb^s Hb^s) form kills 100 000 young people a year. The distribution of this disease in Africa correlates closely with that of an even more powerful killer – malaria – which is still responsible for more deaths than any other pathogenic disease. Study table 3.3, which summarises the information on this condition. In areas of high sickle-cell gene frequency such as West Africa, up to 4% of the population may be born anaemia sufferers; here malaria is a prevalent disease and has been for centuries. It has been shown that those with sickle-cell *trait* (Hb^A Hb^s) and sickle-cell anaemia (Hb^s Hb^s) are more resistant to malaria. Those without the sickle-cell gene (Hb^A Hb^A) have no ready resistance to malaria. Although sickle-cell anaemics are malaria-resistant, they are likely to die young and, until the advent of recent treatments, relatively few have lived to found a family of their own. In 1976, Bodmer and Cavalli-Sforza computed the relative fitness of individuals on the basis of blood typing and mortality rates from malaria and sickle-cell in a population where blood types were

Table 3.3 Data on sickle-cell anaemia in the Yoruba population of Ibadan, Nigeria

Genotype	Hb^AHb^A	Hb^AHb^s	Hb^sHb^s
Phenotype	normal	sickle-cell trait	sickle-cell anaemia
Blood performance characteristic	normal	normal	anaemic
Malaria resistance	low	high	high
Relative fitness	0.85	1.00	0.10
Genotype frequency (%) in the population at birth	76.92	21.57	1.51
Genotype frequency (%) in adults	75.60	24.16	0.24

Source: Bodmer, W. F. and Cavalli-Sforza, L. L., *Genetics, evolution and man*, W. H. Freeman 1976

being screened. It will be seen from table 3.3 that it is the high relative fitness of the heterozygote survivors which continually contributes to the high frequency of sickle-cell genes in the population.

3.8 The mating system

Much of population genetics is based on the assumption that mating between individuals is random. Is this true of our species? Would non-random mating affect the frequency of genes and would the influence be important?

Within a gene pool, more frequent mating between close relatives than would occur by chance is termed **inbreeding**. Some isolated human populations may become inbred and this may contribute to the development of distinguishing features of a local population. Laboratory mice that are brother–sister mated for 20 generations will become a genetically uniform line, being homozygous at every gene locus. Such situations in nature must be rare. Almost all human societies have taboos about sex between close relatives. Brother–sister marriages are rarely encouraged in any social system, though they did occur in the royal households of the Incas and the Ptolemies.

In contrast, if matings occur less frequently between closely related individuals then **outbreeding** occurs. Most sexually reproducing organisms have outbreeding mechanisms. Many mammals have an inbreeding inhibition against their siblings which promotes outbreeding. Wild chimpanzee males seek out females from neighbouring groups and females often leave or are abducted from their own group. Many human traditional tribal customs require men and women to marry into another clan. Heterozygosity usually increases fitness; indeed a **hybrid vigour** is often apparent when outbreeding occurs from previously inbred groups. This is well known to plant and animal breeders. **Migration** is a major outbreeding influence. Advantageous genes may spread across a continent at a speed of many miles per generation. Gene flow could therefore take place right around the world in a few hundred thousand years without humans doing more than wandering to find a mate in a neighbouring community.

Darwin identified **sexual selection** as a most powerful force for evolutionary change. He pointed to the elaborate displays of male birds as an example. Today we know that the size and quality of a peacock's tail is highly significant in peahen mate choice. A male with fewer 'eyes' in his tail (or even with a small asymmetry) has a far reduced chance of being a father. Not only may males need to compete with each other for mates by mutual aggression, but they may express a preference for individual female partners too. Equally females may rival each other for male partners and, with a choice of males, exercise their choice as well. Mate selection is a large and complex area of behavioural ecology.

Among primates and hominid fossils there is often **sexual dimorphism**, males displaying differing body size and proportions to those of females. The large canines in male apes are an example. Many anthropologists are convinced that sexual selection has been a driving force in human evolution as powerful as the adaptations to environment driven by ordinary natural selection (see sections 10.7 and 11.6). In modern humans it is often found that mating is clearly assortative in measurable ways; people in Britain are more likely to have partners of comparable height, social status and intelligence than random choice would dictate. Similarly, in Britain, red-haired people are less likely to partner red-haired people than random chance would dictate. Such behaviours are complex.

3.9   Small sample effects

Statistically it is well known that biases enter into small samples. To have a significantly 'good' sample it is usual to take at least 50–100 measurements. For this probabilistic reason sample effects in small interbreeding populations can cause a breakdown of the Hardy–Weinberg equilibrium so that the gene frequency will not stay constant from one generation to another. If the frequency of genes in a small population changes markedly from one generation to another it is described as **genetic drift**. If a population falls to below ten individuals it is very likely that rarer alleles will be lost. If the population builds up again there may be a reduced genetic variability from the original population. Such drift may account for differences between small island populations. Where a population has rebuilt itself from a very small genetic base, genetic markers, in the form of rare alleles, may be amplified out of all proportion. The following might be considered as examples of such **founder effects**. Most human populations have a mix of blood types A, B, AB and O, yet some Amerindian tribes in Brazil have only O group blood. In Australia 432 known carriers of Huntington's chorea can trace their ancestry to just one woman colonist who left England with 13 children. In South Africa the original Afrikaner population of South Africa was established very largely by one boatload of immigrants in 1652. Of the 2.5 million Afrikaners in South Africa today, 1 million have a surname the same as just 20 of the immigrants on that ship.

Questions to think about

1   Research Jean Baptiste Lamarck's theory of evolution. He proposed two axioms, the 'Law of use and disuse' and the 'Law of inheritance of acquired characteristics'. What would need to happen at the cellular level if Lamarck's theory were true?

2   What evolutionary change is only due to selection mechanisms and what is due to chance mechanisms alone?

3   Given the variation in modern humans, debate in your class the significance of sexual selection in human evolution.

The record of the rocks

4.1 Palaeontology

Fossil evidence for human origins has built up steadily during the twentieth century. As a young man Darwin was a fossil hunter and a pioneer biogeographer. He proved to his own satisfaction that South America once had now long-extinct mammals. The fossilised skeletons he excavated in Argentina were completely new to science and their form showed clear anatomical links to the living fauna of that same region. Darwin was later so confident in his biogeographical science that he predicted, on the basis of the gorilla and chimpanzee living in Africa, that it would be in that continent that hominid fossils would be found. Africa was then barely explored by Europeans. Although fossil humans have been found throughout the world, it is in Africa that the earliest hominid finds have been made – Darwin guessed right.

Today **palaeontology**, the study of fossils, is a well-developed science, calling on widespread areas of expertise. Human fossils are few and fragmentary and nowhere easily found. This makes **palaeoanthropology**, the study of human fossils, most demanding and difficult. Discovery, excavation, dating, reconstructing, cataloguing and naming are just the start. Interpretation is all-important.

4.2 The restless Earth

Most of us live with the feeling that the Earth beneath our feet is solid and dependable. Only in an earthquake, flood, tidal wave or volcanic eruption is one's faith shaken somewhat. Several of Darwin's immediate predecessors were great geologists who helped develop our modern concept of **geological time**. James Hutton, the founder of geological science, deduced that rocks are a product of processes still going on today: vulcanism, inundation by the sea, weathering, erosion and sedimentation, and so on. He established the principle that any sedimentary or igneous rocks overlying deeper bedded rocks will be of a younger age. Charles Lyell, Darwin's geologist mentor, used the fossil sea shells of the strata to date contemporary rocks in different localities and, on the basis of their bedding and their fossil fauna, was able to date older and younger rocks. Lyell recognised the origin of new fossil forms and the terminal extinction of species. Adam Sedgwick, a Cambridge professor of geology who went on field excursions with Darwin, showed how the rocks of the west of Britain were much deeper bedded and more ancient than those in the east (it was Lyell and Sedgwick who devised many of the geological period names, including the Palaeozoic, Cambrian, Devonian, Carboniferous, Cenozoic, Eocene, Pliocene and Miocene). Sedgwick taught Darwin about faulting and uplift. In South America, Darwin found fossil sea shells high in the Andes, lifted from the Pacific ocean floor by colliding crustal plates. So strong was the non-evolutionary thought-frame of their time that Lyell, Sedgwick and Darwin felt only able to push back the age of the Earth from the biblical 4004 BC to an age of about 3 million years. Today we believe that the earliest fossils were formed over 3.5 *thousand* million years ago and that the Earth is another thousand million years older than that.

There are key pieces of geological and geoclimatic knowledge that help us to understand human evolution. **Tectonic plate movements**, driven by convection currents in the Earth's mantle, were important in separating the Americas from Africa 60 million years ago. This Atlantic divide separated the Old World and New World primates from each other. Each group evolved quite separately. Tectonic **rift faulting** and **uplift** have been of major importance in East Africa, where the Great Rift Valley has been the site of most hominid fossil finds. Frequent volcanic events and rift valley lake bed sediments have ensured an almost uninterrupted fossil record spanning millions of years.

Over the full extent of geological time there have been some large discontinuities. The Earth's magnetic field is oriented by its metallic core. The dipole of this huge magnet oscillates, so that the poles move continually. Periodically there are complete **geomagnetic reversals** of the pole (the compass needle points south instead of north). We do not know how or why this happens, but all eruptions of igneous rocks containing iron retain a lasting record of the prevailing geomagnetism as they cool and solidify.

There are large **extinction episodes** in the fossil record at the end of the Ordovician, Devonian, Permian, Triassic and Cretaceous periods. These extinctions, when whole families of animals and plants disappeared, often made ecological space for the biological radiation of new living forms to develop. The Permian extinction of 220 million years ago was massive; that at the end of the Cretaceous 65 million years ago caused the dinosaurs to die out. This catastrophe may have been due to an asteroid or comet impact. From that date the mammals and the ancestors of the primates grew in importance.

Climate was not always the same in geological history as it is now. Mean global temperatures have declined in the last 50 million years. Early in the evolution of the primates, tropical rain forest was widespread throughout the world. But since the mid-Miocene the climate has become drier and woodlands and savannahs have become more extensive. Small forest-living antelopes evolved into woodland forms, and large savannah herbivores like horses appeared for the first time. This was the environment of the first upright walking apes. Within the general drying trend were cyclic fluctuations of temperature and rainfall, and as the climate shifted, the response of forms adapted to the new, drier environments would be to migrate. With each cyclic fluctuation in global temperature the ice sheets have expanded and contracted. There was a major cold period 5 million years ago at a time when the first hominids appeared. There was also a second cold period 2.4 million years ago at the time when the genus *Homo* arose, and the bonobo (*Pan paniscus*) may have separated from the other chimp species at this time. There have been periodic **ice-ages** for at least the last 1.5 million years. The ice-ages of the most recent 100 000 years had a dramatic impact on human form and culture, only coming to an end 12 000 years ago. During all this time, the accretion and melting of ice has had a dramatic impact on sea-level. During the past 1.5 million years the sea has sometimes been nearly 200 metres lower than it is now. Britain was not then an island. But 35 million years ago, before the great ice sheets at the poles began to form, the sea was perhaps 200 metres higher than it is today. Such **changes in sea-level** make bridges between continents and islands appear and disappear. Together with the advance and retreat of climatic regions and the formation of sea and desert barriers, these have had huge effects on animal and plant movements and the origin of species. It might have been in one of the drier periods or colder periods that hominids first ventured out of Africa.

4.3 Fossilisation

How remains come to be fossilised at all and the circumstances surrounding the process is one of the newest fields in palaeontology. It is called **taphonomy**. Much depends on the events surrounding the death of an animal. Dismemberment by carnivores and scavengers is extremely likely; **bones** may be scattered, trampled, gnawed and crushed by teeth and dispersed over long distances as scavengers take them to their lairs. Weathering agents such as wind, heat, frost, acid water and river erosion may degrade bones rapidly. Taphonomic studies of what happens to animal corpses in the wild have helped greatly with interpreting fossil remains. What is quite clear is that rapid burial, in lake sediments, mud or volcanic ash, is most likely to produce complete fossil individuals. The 'Turkana boy' (*Homo erectus*) discovered in 1984 on the west side of Lake Turkana, in the Kenyan Rift Valley, was rapidly buried in a lagoon sediment 1.5 million years ago; only some few limb bones and small hand and foot bones were missing (see figure 10.3). More commonly only tantalisingly small fragments remain. Many fossils are described from a jaw fragment alone. **Teeth** are of great importance in palaeontology because of their hardness and hence permanence as fossils.

Once surrounded by fine soil particles, bones will be subject to various processes, most of which lead to decay. The protein proceeds to decay and gives an index of age as it goes. The mineral content may decrease in acidic conditions, or be increasingly added to, especially in alkaline conditions. Molecular substitution of bone calcium by other salts, such as silicates, occurs. A fossil may end up much heavier than a bone and may also be distorted by the mass of sediment in which it is crushed. Caves in limestone provide excellent fossilisation sites, for the litter of bones from human or carnivore occupation is bedded in an ideal environment for **mineralisation**. The advent of ritual burial by humans, from perhaps 50 000 years ago, has been of enormous value to more recent archaeology.

Soft parts of early humans are completely unknown as fossils. All artists' reconstructions are thus very tentative and based upon anatomical analysis of old muscle attachment sites on fossil bone. The rare preservation of human flesh has happened in the process of mummification and dehydration (in Egyptian tombs), in acid peat bogs (Danish bog people) and in ice (the famous ice-men and ice-maidens).

4.4 Traces and artefacts

Other remains and traces may be important. Firstly, actual fossil footprints of early hominids are known from Laetoli in Tanzania 3.7 million years ago (see figure 7.7). Artefacts (objects fashioned by people) such as stone tools and pottery also add enormously to evidence of early human existence. These are most important in interpreting cultural evolution. Manufacturing or kill sites, where communities once left their tools and refuse behind, reveal not only the secrets of tool manufacture but also the use to which tools were put, such as cutting meat from bones, digging for plant roots or hammering. Sometimes the marks left by cutting or hammering tool use are found on fossilised animal bones at a site, even if there are no human fossils with them.

4.5 Excavation

The excavation of fossils and artefacts requires the excavator to have a real understanding of past geological events. Reading the rocks is an art as well as a science. If you walk the ground with a geologist in the Great Rift Valley of Africa a story often unfolds. This great scar across the face of Africa is the most outstanding single location for fossils of early humans anywhere in the world (see figure 4.1). The series of faults, caused as the crustal plates moved apart, produced diverging and converging valleys running for 4000 miles from Syria through the Red Sea, Ethiopia and the countries of East Africa all the way to the Zambesi Valley and the Mozambique coast. For many

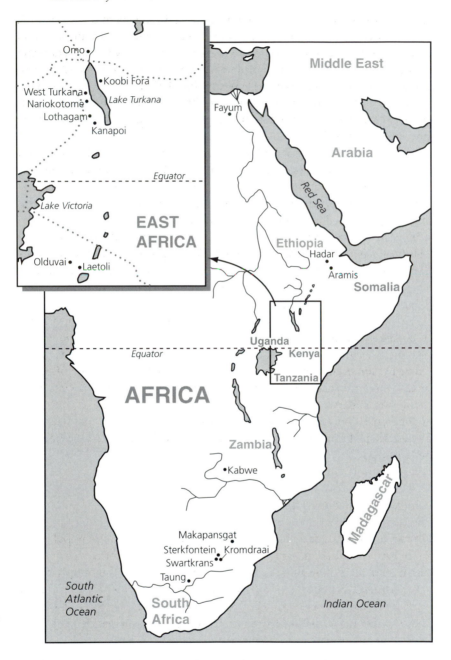

Figure 4.1   The location of important fossil sites in Africa

millions of years the down-faulting and upward movement has continued. Volcanoes have come and gone. Valley bottom lakes have formed and drained many times and expanded and contracted with the changing seasons and climatic periods. Volcanic ash and lava flows of basalt or conglomerate are found sandwiched between the lake bed sediments in the rock strata. Here the record of more than 4 million years of human evolution is interred, although only a fraction has yet been unearthed and a minute amount is described.

A new fossil site is found where erosion of fossil beds by wind and rain exposes them to the air. Because of their hardness the fossils accumulate at the bottom of eroded slopes. This is often where the palaeontologist first finds them and where **excavations** may be planned and begun. The site is first mapped fully. Louis Leakey, the pioneer of African palaeoanthropology in the 1940s, found numerous sites on foot. There were no detailed maps and few permanent markers on the ground. Today, precision location with the Global Positioning System (GPS), satellite and aerial photography all ease the problems. The geology is noted carefully and nearby volcanic beds may be used for absolute dating (see section 4.6). After mapping, the surface fossils are picked up, and then the most promising areas of the site are excavated away in a series of blocks on a grid system, down one layer at a time in the bedded plane. Fossils are mapped as they are found and in the process a three-dimensional picture emerges. Fine soil may be sifted for small teeth or flakes of bone, and large fossils may be strengthened with acrylic hardeners, or, if very delicate, cased in plaster for removal to the laboratory. Specimens are then numbered, cleaned with meticulous care using fine dental picks and scrapers, and put aside for full database cataloguing (see section 4.7).

4.6   Dating fossils

Geochronology, the dating of rocks, is of particular importance in palaeoanthropology. The dating, or **time sequencing**, of fossil forms has a huge bearing on their interpretation. You might argue that this emphasis on dating is excessive, but 'once bitten twice shy' has been the motto of every worker in this field since the notorious Piltdown man[1] hoax, which lasted from its 'discovery' in 1912 to its revelation as a fraud some 40 years later,

[1] The Piltdown forgery came to light because of the development of absolute dating methods. The supposed remains came from Pleistocene gravels, near the village of Piltdown in Sussex, in which the associated fauna was clearly not modern. In 1949, when the Piltdown jaw was tested for the accumulation of fluorine, which increases its presence in bones with age, it failed lamentably to match the Pleistocene elephant and mastodont remains, having 15 times less fluorine. The forgery was confirmed in 1953 by evidence of the staining and filing of the jaw to fit what was essentially a modern skull. The jaw belonged to an orang-utan! Radiocarbon dating, carried out in 1959, confirmed the remains as being only a few hundred years old.

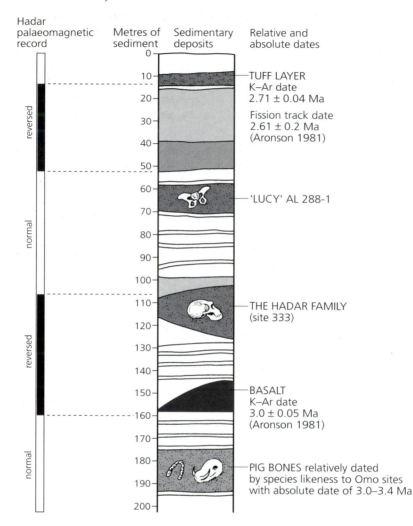

Figure 4.2 Relative and absolute dating of fossil deposits

causing mayhem in the interpretation of remains in the period between. **Direct dating methods** are used on the fossils themselves, whilst **indirect methods** give a date to associated rocks or remains (see figure 4.2).

Relative dating looks at the age of the fossils of one stratum relative to the age of other associated fauna and flora at another site elsewhere. Often there is a local collection of fossils that is abundant and characteristic. For example, species such as mastodonts in Britain or pig species in Africa occur frequently in the fossil record, and their changing form sets a time frame. If the duration of one species' existence is known from one good site, remains found elsewhere and contemporary with those of a hominid may give the latter a relative date. The bones of one horizon should be alike in chemical composition. However, often fossils may be washed out of a higher horizon and buried in a lower one, hence making them appear older than they really are. In a volcanic region palaeomagnetism may provide a relative date from the magnetic field at the time of eruption, as fixed in cooled lava. Palaeomagnetic recording of whether a rock has a normal or reversed magnetism may help to settle a date in conjunction with other methods.

Absolute dating involves the use of physicochemical methods to estimate absolute ages. The earliest rough method was the accumulation of fluorine in bones as a direct method indicator of their age. Today most absolute methods are radiometric, employing the fact that radioactive isotopes decay exponentially with time and do so independently of temperature and pressure. **Radiocarbon dating** was invented first; this is based on the decay of carbon-14 to carbon-12. The carbon-14 isotope is formed in the atmosphere from carbon-12. Once fixed into organic matter it decays slowly at a fixed declining rate (halving every 5.76×10^3 years). The carbon-14 level may be accurately detected on direct analysis of a very small fragment. This test gives good dates for the last 60 000 years. **Potassium–argon dating** (^{40}K–^{40}Ar) is useful for spanning all of geological time back to the Cambrian, but is too slow to be used for the most recent half million years. Exactly 0.001118% of the Earth's potassium is currently found as isotope ^{40}K. This decays to the inert gas argon ^{40}Ar (with a half-life of 1.28×10^9 years). When volcanic lava is hot all the argon escapes, but in solidified lava the argon gas molecules produced by continuing decay are trapped. Analysis of small samples of volcanic rock may show their age from the amount of ^{40}Ar they contain. The time-scale gap between these dating methods is filled by three techniques of slightly lower reliability. The first is **fission track dating**. Volcanic glass (obsidian) often contains uranium-238. The fission of the isotope leaves a track through the glass, so that the older it is the more microscopic fission tracks may be counted. Similarly, the decay of uranium isotopes causes electrons to be emitted into the crystal lattice. These may either be detected by seeing how much light they emit when released from

Table 4.1 The relative usefulness of absolute dating methods

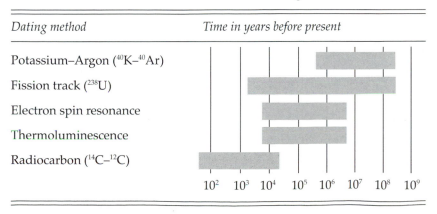

Dating method	Time in years before present
Potassium–Argon (^{40}K–^{40}Ar)	
Fission track (^{238}U)	
Electron spin resonance	
Thermoluminescence	
Radiocarbon (^{14}C–^{12}C)	
	10^2 10^3 10^4 10^5 10^6 10^7 10^8 10^9

the rock on heating (**thermoluminescence**) or they may be detected in situ by measuring **electron spin resonance**. These latter techniques cover the time-span between a few thousand years and 1 million years ago (see table 4.1).

We know that flint and pottery lose their electron spin resonance on heating. This re-sets the 'timer' to zero. Such is the technological skill behind absolute dating that either a flint arrowhead or a fired pot heated in antiquity may be dated by the thermoluminescence that will have built up since that heating event. Generally a site can be fairly easily dated; some, however, like Kromdraai, Makapansgat and Sterkfontein in South Africa, present peculiar problems because there are no associated volcanic rocks and the hominid remains have fallen out of all easily interpreted order into limestone fissures and caves.

4.7 Analysis of remains

The analysis of fossil collections is exacting work. For each fossil the following are written down and data-banked:

1 an alphabetical letter code and number (e.g. Johanson's famous 'Lucy' (see section 8.3) is AL 288-1);
2 assignation to the lowest (smallest) taxonomic position that can be given with confidence;
3 anatomical nature and degree of tooth wear (e.g. left humerus, upper half only);
4 locality number and site position;
5 taphonomic indicators (e.g. abrasion, weathering, toothmarks, evidence of disease);
6 size measurements of the specimen.

Such data collection makes computer-based searches for comparable material easier and also allows for statistical analysis of many different specimens. Analysis of such large amounts of data enables generalisations to be made in the discussion and interpretation of results. Many challenges then follow. Reconstructed crania may have their volumes measured. Endocasts of the cranium reveal not only brain volume but also the brain lobe regions that are developed. Dietary studies come from teeth; even the microwear of the tooth enamel examined by a scanning electron microscope may reveal what sort of food a hominid ate.

Questions to think about

1 Have you ever unearthed a fossil? How was it fossilised? What can you tell about the life of that organism from the rock it came from?

2 If the whole of the time since life developed on Earth (3.5 billion years ago) was equivalent to just one year of real time, calculate what periods of history would be fitted into the last minute and last second before midnight on the last day of that year.

3 Why does dating so affect interpretation of the fossil record?

FIVE

Our living record

5.1 The living evidence for evolution

When asked for the evidence for evolution most of us think of fossils. However, there is equally brilliant evidence for evolution within the bodies of living things. This is apparent at the anatomical level down to the molecular. Every new individual is on an ancestral developmental pathway – followed successfully a myriad of times before – but the path is always slightly changed. Separate species deriving from one distant common ancestor are today on different tracks. Every species is at the end of its branch in the 'tree of life'. Once you adopt this Linnaean tree of branching relatedness with its Darwinian perception of 'descent with modification', comparative studies between the ends of the living branches take on new meaning. This chapter is concerned with this living evidence.

5.2 Comparative anatomy

Zoologists often compare the anatomy of one form with another, to develop an understanding of why animals are adapted as they are and the extent to which their shape and form reflect their evolutionary relatedness. Where two branch ends are alike we might see it as a convergence due to a similar adaptation or, on the other hand, as a similarity explained by a descent from a common ancestor. A shark, a salmon, a penguin and a dolphin all have a highly streamlined shape. This hydrodynamic adaptation enables them to move quickly through water and is based on a functional requirement for speed; streamlining produces **analogous structures** that serve a common functional purpose. Other similarities between animal forms are less easily explained by functionalism. The classic example is the pentadactyl (five-fingered) limb. All land-living tetrapods (four-limbed animals) have this feature in common by virtue of their common descent. Amphibians, reptiles, birds and mammals all develop (at least embryonically) a five-fingered hand and foot. This is a **homologous structure**. In the limb there is a single upper limb bone, two lower limb bones, a number of carpals and five terminal digits. This shared descent homology is often disguised in the diverse adaptations of the limb. As Darwin remarked, 'What could be more curious than that the

(a)

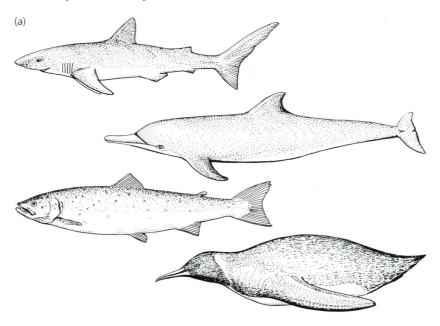

(b)   Human   Bird   Whale   Bat

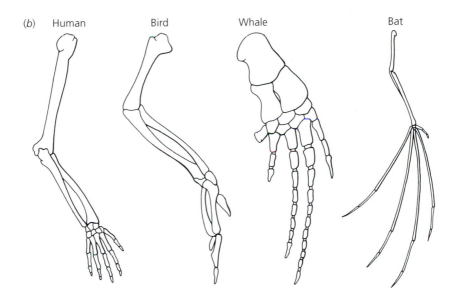

Figure 5.1   Analogy and homology. (a) Many aquatic vertebrate groups display a hydrodynamic shape, an analogous structural adaptation to swimming in water. (b) The limb bones of a human, a bird, a whale and a bat, though different in function, are all alike in basic structure.

hand of man formed for grasping, that of a mole for digging, the leg of a horse, the paddle of a porpoise, and the wing of a bat, should all be constructed on the same pattern and should include similar bones in the same positions?'

Compelling evidence for evolution comes from homologous **vestigial organs**. Snakes and whales have no external hind limbs at all; homology helps to explain the pelvic girdle bones and femur of the python and the whale. In our large intestine, the colonic appendix serves no useful function, yet a functional fermentation chamber is a feature of the guts of the other large primates. If functionalism was to rule entirely, none of the homologous anomalies that we sometimes find would exist. Appreciating the difference between analogy and homology compels us to question whether any similarity in evolution is due to convergence or, alternatively, is evidence of a common descent.

5.3   Embryos and ancestors

The German biologist Ernst Haeckel (1834–1919), an early Darwinian advocate, made extensive embryological studies of vertebrates and claimed that the development of zygotes through embryo to adult repeated the pathway of evolutionary development from protozoan to modern vertebrate. This is the **theory of recapitulation**. There is only a partial element of truth in it, since embryos adapt to their environment as adults do, but there are compelling homologies between the early stages of vertebrate embryos which we cannot ignore. At a few weeks old, the human embryo has a well developed tail and gill slits in the pharynx wall, like an embryo fish. At a much later stage of human development a complete covering of fine body hair forms all over the foetus, only to be shed before birth.

5.4   Comparative biochemistry

If anatomical features show similarity, so too do biochemical features. ATP and DNA are universal in their roles in all organisms. Within the DNA code a triplet might in theory read for any of the twenty amino acids, since there is no fundamental chemical reason to match a particular triplet to a particular amino acid. Yet the actual coding is adhered to because the enzymes that control the union of specific amino acids only latch on to transfer RNA molecules with specific triplets on them. These ancient enzymes are totally homologous, making the code universal for all forms of life. The gene coding for vertebrate haemoglobin is similar in all vertebrates and found only in these animals. Yet insertion of a human code messenger RNA for haemoglobin into the bacterium *Escherichia coli* results in the bacterium making that human protein. The universal **homology of the genetic code**, reflecting an originally slender stem to the whole tree of life, is what makes genetic engineering a possibility.

5.5   Protein sequences

During the 1950s, Frederick Sanger eventually succeeded in working out the sequence of the amino acids in just one short protein, insulin. This was a major breakthrough; by the 1960s this had become an easier thing to do. The first application of this technology was in medical research, chasing the products of faulty genes such as sickle-cell haemoglobin. It was suggested by Linus Pauling and Emil Zuckerkandl in 1962 that amino acid sequencing was a powerful tool for looking at molecular homology and rates of evolution. It was suggested that the accumulation of mutational change since the separation of different evolutionary lines, such as birds, reptiles and mammals, might be used as a measure of the evolutionary distance between them. In such lineages the homologous molecules, like cytochrome and haemoglobin, were known from electrophoretic studies to differ slightly. Zuckerkandl had discovered that gorilla haemoglobin was only one amino acid different from human haemoglobin. Amino acid sequences of blood proteins of several animals more widely separated in evolutionary terms were examined. It became clear that the same functional molecule in two different animals did indeed differ in amino acid sequence roughly in pro-portion to the time since their lines might have separated. By the late 1960s, many molecular biologists had accepted the hypothesis of a **molecular clock** ticking away to produce regular change in molecules. If such a clock existed it would be useful in sorting out evolutionary relationships, for the molecular clock could be calibrated against the new absolute potassium–argon dates from the geological record (see section 4.6). In 1970 Walter Fitch and Emmanuel Margoliash worked on the cytochrome *c* sequence of 20 different organisms; in trying to work out the truest relation-ship, they applied the principle that one should reduce to a minimum the number of assumptions made. (This philosophical idea is known as the Maximum Parsimony Principle, the Law of Parsimony or 'Occam's Razor'.) They sketched out a branch diagram (cladogram) based on the smallest number of differences in the genetic code that would be required to account for the different sequences between the species (see section 6.4). This simplest or **most parsimonious relationship** agreed substantially with the branching diagram of anatomical homology with which biologists were already in general agreement.

At this point it is important to ask whether protein amino acid sequences change in response to natural selection or in a random process that could be expected to happen at a more or less constant rate. This is still an area of controversy in modern evolutionary biology. Motoo Kimura initially thought that the random rate of amino acid substitution was fairly constant for all proteins and had suggested a **neutral theory** (see section 3.4) to explain such change, acting independently of natural selection. The chance of one amino acid changing was initially estimated as once in 2.8

billion years. Since proteins have hundreds of specific amino acid sites in sequence, at least some would be expected to change, with changed DNA coding, over relatively few millions of years. Table 5.1 shows the variation that Kimura has since recorded and it is clearly very varied. Some molecules that are probably quite ancient, like the cytochromes (in mitochondria) and the histones (which package DNA in chromosomes), have altered little. Others, like the fibrinopeptides (concerned with blood clotting), have changed more.

The rate of change in the shape and adaptations of animals in the course of evolution is certainly not constant. Some animals, like sharks, have not changed in 300 million years. Most **selectionists** would have said that the shark's almost unchanging environment should result in little evolutionary change in the species. To counter this natural selectionist argument Kimura studied shark and human blood. His neutral drift theory would predict that they are both changing at the molecular level. Haemoglobin has two different globins, an α-chain and a β-chain. All vertebrates have evolved their complex globins from the early ancestors of all vertebrates. Kimura argued that if, contrary to neutral drift, shark haemoglobin had not been evolving as quickly, then the amount of difference between their α- and β-globins would be much less than that of humans. The number of amino acid differences between the chains in humans is 147 amino acids, that for the shark 150. This seems to confirm his neutral drift idea for one class of proteins: the haemoglobin clock seems to tick regularly. But why are different proteins so different in their rates of change (see table 5.1)? We now know that the functional parts of a protein's amino acid sequence are less likely to alter over time. Thus pro-insulin, the precursor of insulin, has a section that is cut out before the molecule becomes active. The rate of amino

Table 5.1   Rate of evolution in eight proteins; the rates are expressed as random numbers of amino acid changes per amino acid site in 10^9 years.

Protein	Rate (number of changes in 10^9 years)
Fibrinopeptides	8.3
Pancreatic ribonuclease	2.1
Lysozyme	2.0
α-globin	1.2
Myoglobin	0.89
Insulin	0.44
Cytochrome *c*	0.3
Histone H4	0.01

Source: Kimura, M., *The neutral theory of molecular evolution*,
Cambridge University Press 1983

acid change in this part is six times faster than in the functional region. In haemoglobin the haem pocket, containing the active site, is extremely conservative and hardly changes, whereas the outer chains of the haemoglobin molecule vary most. Mutations in the active site will have large effects and those outside will have smaller ones. This 'selectionist' view seems to explain the different rates of molecular evolution shown in table 5.1.

5.6 Immuno-relatedness

It has long been understood that our bodies recognise foreign proteins. On the outside of a human blood protein like albumin there are 30 or 40 sites that can be recognised by antibodies. Immunologists recognise that the degree of the antibody–antigen reaction, which produces a chemical precipitation, relates to the degree to which there are such antigen sites onto which antibodies can latch. As we do not make antibodies for our own proteins, the **immunological reaction** is therefore the greater if a protein is more different from those normally present in the body. In 1963 Morris Goodman began to investigate the immunological differences between the great apes and humans and established to his surprise that the orang-utan is more different in its blood proteins from chimpanzees and gorillas than chimpanzees and gorillas are from humans. Gauging such an immunological reaction is much easier than protein sequencing.

This immunological research inspired Allan Wilson and Vincent Sarich to produce (in 1966) what is perhaps the best-known piece of research on **molecular clocks**. Sarich and Wilson decided to investigate albumin, a very species-specific blood protein. Human blood albumin has 584 amino acids and a complex molecular shape. Antibodies are only made in the living body, so to prepare antibodies to human albumin the experimenters injected the human blood protein into a rabbit, collecting the rabbit anti-human albumin antisera about two months later. This contained some 30–40 different anti-human albumin antibodies. Working *in vitro*, they then gauged

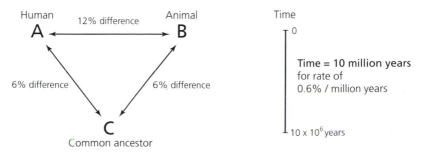

Figure 5.2 The human albumin immuno-distance clock. The molecular clock envisages a common ancestor of two living forms as being half as different, in terms of molecular evolution. The clock is set to a known geochronological date.

the degree of precipitation with albumin from humans (100% reaction) and the sera from nine other animals (see table 5.2). Sarich and Wilson argued that if this was a constant biological clock then the percentage immuno-difference between humans and one of these animals should reflect the sum of the molecular clock differences back to a common ancestor plus the sum of the clock differences forward to the present (see figure 5.2). As we don't know the common ancestor (and its blood is untestable!) the difference between two forms is halved to gauge the difference between the modern form and the ancestor. The radiation of the order Primates is known geochronologically to have occurred some 60 million years ago. As a precip-itation of 30% or more would include all primates from the lemurs upwards, a total 70% change (i.e. 100% minus 30%) could be split 35% back to a common ancestor and 35% forward to a modern form. This gives the molecular clock a forward rate of 35% change in 60 million years, or approx-imately 0.6% every million years. When these immuno-distances are converted into millions of years, the surprise is the apparent closeness of humans to the chimpanzee and the gorilla.

Despite the fact that none of Sarich and Wilson's conclusions conflict with the fossil evidence, some palaeontologists still distrust these molecular methods.

Table 5.2 Immuno-relatedness of humans and various mammals on the basis of percentage precipitation of each of the animal albumins with rabbit anti-human albumin antibodies. (See text for explanation of the calculation of 'molecular clock' values in millions of years.)

Species tested with the anti-human albumin antibody	Precipitation of the species albumin with anti-human albumin antibody (%)	Difference from human (%)	Difference to common ancestor (%) (half difference from human)	Postulated time since common ancestor (million years)
Human (control)	100	0	0	0
Chimpanzee	95	5	2.5	4
Gorilla	95	5	2.5	4
Orang-utan	85	15	7.5	13
Gibbon	82	18	9	15
Baboon	73	27	13.5	23
Spider monkey	60	40	20	34
Ruffed lemur	35	65	32.5	55
Dog	25	75	37.5	64
Kangaroo	8	92	46	79

Source: data from Ridley, M., *Evolution*, Blackwell Scientific Publications 1993

5.7   DNA sequences

Underlying all of these homologies is DNA. Frederick Sanger, who was awarded a Nobel prize in 1958 for the first sequencing of a protein, achieved a 'double' by receiving a second Nobel prize, 20 years later, for being the first to sequence DNA! Today DNA sequencing is a mechanised routine activity. We know the entire genetic sequence not only of single genes, but of several entire small organisms as well. The project running at the **Human Genome Organisation** (HuGO) has been built round the technology and we now have an immense amount of genome data on our own species. This could be of immeasurable benefit. There is no reason (other than cost) why in the future there should not be a genome project for any other organism, great apes included.

DNA–DNA hybridisation is another molecular method of exploring our living evolutionary record. When heated, DNA molecules 'melt' to a single-stranded form which will then zip up with complementary strands if placed in a solution. The better matched the strands are, the stronger the zipping and, if strongly hydrogen-bonded along the helix, the less likely they are to disengage at a subsequently increased temperature. In 1987 Charles Sibley and John Ahlquist used this fact to develop a method employing the DNA of one species to find matching complementary sequences of DNA in another species, and so obtain a measure of relatedness by the degree to which the hybridisation forms and holds. This is essentially parallel to Sarich's work but is more finely tuned to looking at smaller differences. Sibley used 17 temperatures from 55 °C to 95 °C in 2.5 °C increments. Using radioactively labelled DNA he recorded the temperature at which half of the hybridised DNA is paired (ΔT_{50H}). The more similar the DNA samples are, the higher the temperature of the hybridisation that will hold. As in Sarich's work, the DNA–DNA hybridisation 'clock' is set from geochronology. Estimates of the value for ΔT_{50H} therefore vary between 3.6 and 4.4 million years per 1.0 °C. The results of this investigation are shown in figure 5.3. This places the human–chimpanzee divergence distance (based on the ΔT_{50H} value being 1.6 °C cooler) at between 5.8 and 7.1 million years ago. This kinship is more distant than that suggested by Sarich but is still more recent than many palaeontologists had previously guessed. What is also interesting in this data is the 8–10-million-year separation that it suggests between gorillas and chimpanzees, although other DNA studies have put the kinship of these two great apes much closer together.

Mitochondrial DNA has a high rate of mutation. This may be because the mitochondria lack the repair systems that protect DNA in the nucleus. Mitochondrial plasmids (circular DNA chromosomes) were first base-sequenced in 1981 and have approximately 16 500 base pairs. This material is certainly ideal for working out the patterns of descent from species that have common ancestors from less than 15 million years ago. The problem

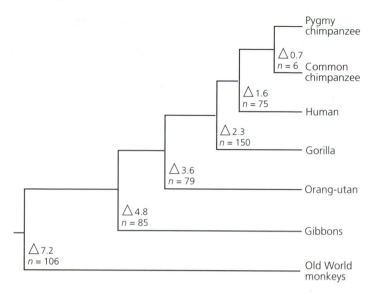

Figure 5.3 DNA–DNA hybridisation evidence: n = sample size for each test; Δ = average ΔT_{50H} value for DNA–DNA comparison. For identical DNAs the value is 0.0. The higher the temperature difference value of Δ becomes, the more dissimilar the molecules are. $\Delta 1.0$, a difference of 1 °C, is roughly equivalent to an evolutionary separation of 4 million years.

with using mitochondrial DNA for dating human and ape divergences is that the anchoring evidence is missing until the relationship is too ancient for the reliability of the method. It again points to a human–chimpanzee divide between 4 and 10 million years ago (see figure 5.4). Mitochondrial DNA as a molecular clock has recently come to prominence with discussion of the **'African Eve' hypothesis** – the notion that all modern humans emerged very recently 'out of Africa'. This is discussed in section 11.5. However, **molecular anthropology** is a science still in its infancy.

5.8   The structure of chromosomes

Chromosomes have a century of good study behind them. If human or animal cells are grown in culture and blocked by a mitotic inhibitor at metaphase and then stained, they may be examined in detail under a light microscope. If you were to do this, you would find that baboons have 42 chromosomes, humans 46 and chimpanzees and gorillas 48. One of the features of chromosomes that enables cytologists to look for chromosome anomalies, like Down's syndrome, is that staining produces characteristic banding patterns. These patterns are so standard that a chromosome may

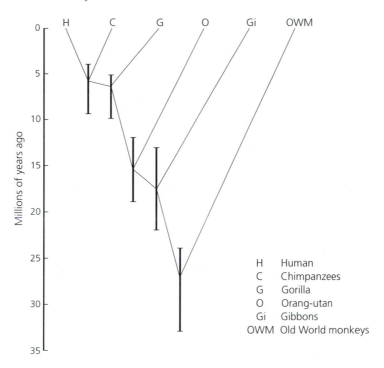

Figure 5.4 An evolutionary tree for primates based on globin and mitochondrial gene sequences. The pattern represents a consensus of recent studies, but the relationships between humans, chimpanzees and gorillas remain questionable. The bars indicate ranges of estimated times for the branch points. (See also figure 7.1)

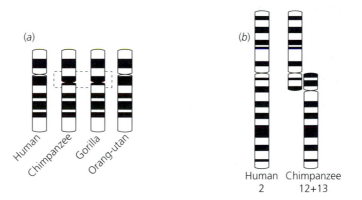

Figure 5.5 Chromosome evidence for relatedness of the great apes. (a) G-banded chromosome 12 of humans, and its homologues in chimpanzees, gorillas and orangutans, reveals a small inversion shared by chimpanzees and gorillas; (b) the large human chromosome 2 is the result of a fusion of two smaller chromosomes still possessed by all great apes; the G bands of chimpanzee chromosomes 12 and 13 match up almost perfectly with the short and long arms, respectively, of human 2; the additional material on the short arm of each of the chimpanzee homologues was added subsequent to the fusion in the human line.

almost be read like a bar-coded sequence. Why, if we are so closely related to the chimpanzee, do they have a whole chromosome set extra? A study of the banding pattern reveals that one of the largest chromosomes in our line-up, chromosome 2, is a fusion of two middle-sized ones, chromosomes 12 and 13, of the chimpanzee (see figure 5.5).

The homologies between these chromosomes are impressive. Huge areas of banding are similar between the great apes and ourselves, though on human chromosome 1 there is a duplication that is not found in the chimpanzee. At this cellular level the chromosomes provide a record of the way in which the genetic material has been rearranged over very long periods of time. On the homologue of human chromosome 12 in the African apes there is a small chromosomal inversion, a turn-around of a short length in the banding pattern, which we lack (see figure 5.5). This would link the chimp and gorilla more closely together than hybridisation evidence suggests; so cytogenetic studies are ambivalent on the detail of human and great ape affinities. When the Human Genome Project is completed there may be better opportunities for tracking down the details of exactly how our chromosome complement and genome came to be.

Questions to think about

1 Distinguish between analogous and homologous features. Why is this an important difference for an evolutionist?

2 It is sometimes said that a chimpanzee is genetically 99% the same as a human being. Is this a helpful statement biologically?

3 Vincent Sarich said, 'I know my molecules had ancestors, but the palaeontologist can only hope that his fossils had descendants.' What is the significance of this remark?

SIX

Thinking about evolution

6.1   The origin of species

This chapter aims to show how species originate and change and how we try
to picture and express that relationship. There are some difficult ideas in this
chapter; but if you are to be a serious student of evolution and if the study of
human evolution is to be a science, and not an uncritically told 'just so' story,
then these ideas must be thought through carefully.

Chapter 3 of this book looked at mechanisms for change that have
resulted in the evolutionary tree of life. What we have not examined is how
new species arise. What is a species? We recognise the different sorts of birds
in our gardens by their definable species characteristics. Members of a
species are certainly very alike and share characteristics between themselves
that mark them off from others. The basis of this similarity is that members
of a species recognise each other, interbreed and thus have a common gene
pool. Species often occupy a particular ecological niche which is usually
closely defined by their adaptation to their environment. New species arise

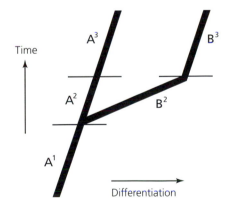

Figure 6.1   Two types of speciation: A^1, A^2, A^3 is a phyletic series of species which, with
respect to time, arose in an anagenic manner. A^1, B^2, B^3 is a second phyletic series, but B^2
has changed more markedly in form than A^2, perhaps as a result of isolation, a branch
has been produced. Such a branching-out origin of species is called cladogenic. A^3 and
B^3 are contemporary species which, through their difference from each other, might
now be genetically isolated if brought together in the same environment.

in one of two possible ways to produce the branching bush structure of the evolutionary tree.

Firstly, over evolutionary time one species may give rise to another through becoming different. Such a gradual phyletic origin of a new species is called **anagenesis** (see A^1, A^2, A^3 in figure 6.1). Even if *Australopithecus*, an early hominid form (see artist's reconstruction, figure 8.2), really was ancestral to ourselves, we should certainly see it as a different species if we met one at a bus stop! The difficulty of defining different species over time is that it is hard to know where to draw the line between one species and the next (see section 6.5). Secondly, true 'speciation' happens at any branching of the evolutionary tree (see A^1, A^2, B^2 in figure 6.1). Here one species must split off from another as a branch; this is called **cladogenesis**. Biologists agree that the only way a branch will form is by the breakdown of what has, up to that moment, held a species together. Some barrier must come between members of a species (such as an uncrossable river, mountain range or sea) or, at the very least, some ecological separation needs to occur. As time goes on and the processes of variation and selection continue in each of the two isolated populations, there will eventually be a time when, should the two group members re-encounter one another, they may no longer be behaviourally or genetically compatible.

There are many evidences of this **species barrier**. If a mare (female horse) and a jack (male) donkey have no other choice in captivity, these two different species may well mate and the resulting offspring will be an infertile hybrid – a mule. Although the mule is alive and strong, it is sterile. More often such close species hybrids are unviable in embryonic life. There is certainly no fertility barrier between any of the great variety of human beings today. We can only guess at whether there was a fertility barrier between our own species and the Neanderthals 50 000 years ago. How far back should our fertility barrier be drawn? It certainly lies between ourselves and the great apes. A hybrid between an ape and human is a real possibility (though deeply unethical to attempt); unquestionably, such a 'human mule' would be infertile.

6.2 Patterns of change

What is the pace of evolution? Is it steady or not? Most of us would now expect species to alter slowly over a long period of time. Such a pattern of slow change is described as **phyletic gradualism** (see figure 6.2). Certainly the fossil record supports this gradualist view. In human evolution we can almost watch through the fossil record an *Australopithecus* species turning slowly into *Homo habilis* and from there into *Homo erectus*. Again, the australopithecines slowly became more robust over 3 million years. But is the pace or tempo always so steady? And why is the fossil record sometimes so seemingly incomplete?

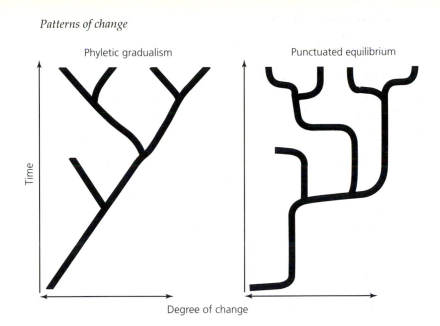

Figure 6.2   Phyletic gradualism and punctuated equilibrium

An answer to both questions was proposed in 1972 when Niles Eldredge and Stephen Jay Gould, who were puzzled by the gaps in the fossil record, suggested that the pace of evolution had different rates from the gradual change which was then accepted: could not the pace be either very fast or really quite slow? On the one hand, they suggested that in the fine tuning of adaptation under environmental constancy a species might not alter very much over quite a long time. This would provide a period of **equilibrium** (with a 'stay as you are' result) and there are many examples of this stability in the fossil record. On the other hand, they argued that when species barriers are set up the isolated forms may well change very quickly, especially in an isolated group. This would show up, for want of fossils, as a break in the fossil record. The equilibrium would be punctuated by sudden change. Darwin recognised the speed with which artificial selection worked and used this as his evidence for the possibility of change; there is no reason to doubt that wild species may be able to change equally fast under natural selection. Eldredge and Gould's **punctuated equilibrium hypothesis** is illustrated in the human story. For instance, *Homo erectus* appears quite suddenly and then changes little in a million years.

The simplest diagrams of evolutionary trees have always been very **monophyletic** with one single 'leading shoot'. Many evolutionists see punctuated equilibrium as making a bush-like structure more possible, where lower branches may suddenly shoot up from below at a faster rate to produce a different leading shoot altogether. Some views on human evolution are more 'bushy'. The suggestion that human forms arose in many branches would be called a **polyphyletic hypothesis**.

6.3 Interpreting growth and form

When we come to look at the changes in the fossil record from one species to another, it is important to ask how those changes may have happened. For example, humans are less hairy, have smaller teeth and are much more brainy than apes. How do such changes occur? The word **allometry** is used to describe the differing measurements of parts of a body in its development or evolution. If the growth of any organism is studied we may identify growth changes where the proportions of the parts vary at different ages. In human development the head grows faster initially and the legs grow faster later on (see figure 6.3). The human thorax and abdomen grow in constant proportion, but the human head grows with a negative allometry (getting relatively smaller) and the legs with a positive allometry (getting relatively bigger). Growth of an individual depends upon the rate of division of cells and the expression of specific genes at a particular age. Wonderful changes in the body form of organisms are possible by merely altering the rate of growth and the timing of the gene switches that affect development. This modification of pace and timing in growth is called **heterochrony**. Often in evolution we find that a new form has a resemblance to an infantile or juvenile form of another species (paedomorphosis). This might be because reproduction is taking place at an earlier age (progenesis), or because the body is not developing to the same pace as the reproductive system (neoteny – see also section 11.6). As we shall see, humans have accelerated their brain growth early in life and delayed their reproductive maturity for longer as

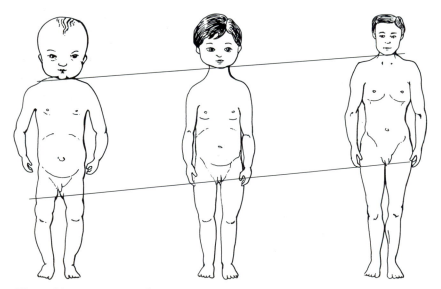

Figure 6.3   Human growth allometry

compared to the apes. Such heterochronic alterations of growth and form are very important features of human evolution and seem to require surprisingly little genetic modification. The concept of major developmental heterochrony in humans supports the evidence for our genetic closeness to the African great apes.

6.4   Seeking the right relationship: phenetics and cladistics

A natural classification should group species according to their degree of physical similarity and so express their evolutionary descent correctly. The problem is that the same characters can appear in a group of species or fossil specimens because of homology and in others because of analogy (see section 5.2). Adaptation of species to environment has a powerful effect in driving some forms convergently together. Wings have evolved separately in insects, bats and birds, but this **parallelism** does not mean that they should be classified together – though we might usefully group them functionally as 'flying animals'. To get the best expression of an evolutionary relationship sorted out we need to ask whether a **phenetic character** (a similar appearance) is found in two different groups because they have converged in finding the same adaptive solution to a similar problem (analogy), or whether the characteristic is the same because of their genetic descent – that is, their common ancestors also had the characteristic (homology). **Phenetic homologies** are what are needed for constructing trees of evolutionary relatedness. A phenetic approach will separate humans considerably from all the great apes on the basis of physical difference. But which characteristics are we to count in looking for similarities and how can we tell the homologies from parallelisms? In 1966 the German entomologist Willi Hennig suggested a solution to the problem using a method he dubbed cladistics.

 Cladistics is a system of analysis of relatedness. It is greatly helped by the use of a computer algorithm for producing the simplest (most parsimonious) relationship between a number of different forms for which a host of

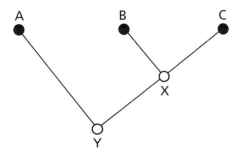

Figure 6.4   A simple cladogram

different characters have been scored as shared or not. The **cladogram** is the resulting branching diagram (see figure 6.4). In a cladistic classification a branched group like ABC in figure 6.4 is called a clade. A, B and C might be modern living forms. We can postulate the existence of X because the number of shared characters between B and C is greater than that between A and B or A and C. We can postulate the existence of Y because of the shared similarities of A, B and C. We have seen in chapter 5 how this method may be used. Using just molecular evidence it is easy to show that the African apes and humans are in the same clade and the orang-utan is in an entirely different group of its own. Does this mean that the African apes and humans should be at least in the same family? Deciding which characters should count for most is difficult and inevitably subjective. Many scientists value cladistic methods because they lend an objectivity to what otherwise may just be only an intuitive feeling. Recent cladistic analysis suggests that the Asian variant of *Homo erectus* cannot be closely grouped with *Homo sapiens*.

6.5 Naming of fossils: splitters and lumpers

The naming of living species, if they are distinct and well-established forms, is relatively easy. But hominid fossils are rudimentary and rare, so their naming has been based on little evidence and is as confusing for the student of evolution as it is contentious for palaeoanthropologists themselves.

A palaeontologist describing a fossil tries to place it into the lowest taxon into which it will fit (see section 2.1). If it is outside the range of known fossils in its range of characters it may be described as a **new species** or even genus if its specific status alone seems to be insufficient to do justice to the specimen's uniqueness. Two factors have encouraged a plethora of namings. Firstly, there were initially insufficient fossils to create the breadth of variation we now expect in any species; each find has seemed unique. Secondly, discoverers often feel so proud of their fossil novelty that new names feel justly deserved at the time. Certainly the media respond to new human remains, and research funding flows more readily with a new name and the attendant publicity. The **splitters**, who tend to give every new find a new name, seem to fragment the picture, but other forces drive things together again. The 'rule of priority' in nomenclature dictates that once a type specimen is described, any subsequent namings that prove to be in the same taxon must conform, unless everyone agrees it is distinctly different. Thus Dubois' named discovery of *Pithecanthropus erectus* in 1891 was later recognised to be in the same genus as ourselves, *Homo* (as named by von Linné). *Pithecanthropus* disappeared into the genus *Homo*, and *Homo erectus* became its species name. The genus *Australopithecus* has absorbed *Zinjanthropus*, *Plesianthropus* and *Paranthropus* for similar reasons. The **lumpers**, who are happy to have a greater diversity of discovered forms within one superspecies, claim that their approach allows a freer discussion of the true phylogenetic relationship. It is interesting that some splitters, who see human evolution proceeding in a very branched and bushy manner, will see a group like *Homo erectus* as so ancient and different from modern *Homo* as to be returned to the genus *Pithecanthropus*. Other lumpers, with affection for chimpanzees and molecular clocks, might even see chimps, humans and all australopithecines as *Homo* and so *Homo sapiens* as a third species of chimpanzee!

6.6 Scenarios and hero myths

The evidence for parts of our evolution story also comes from strands of ecology, physiology, behaviour, palaeoclimatology and a mishmash of other non-fossil evidences that suggest a particular **scenario** in which early humans might have lived. Such a picture may be important and valuable in establishing our thinking about the human story. As we shall see, palaeoanthropologists need to set scenarios to have useful discussions of the evidence, but there is a danger in unsubstantiated scenarios. We also need to be aware of developing too much of a **hero myth** in telling the story. It is too easy to write a folk-tale in which an ancient, heroic ape sets off from the trees into the savannahs of Africa brandishing a wooden club at predators, developing its new-found brain, ingeniously devising tools and developing a social sophistication in which grunts become speech and finally ... civilisation is born! From our vantage point in the present, when we can view the outcome, it is tempting to cling on to this old, progressivist picture. We should be careful not to suggest the causes or origins of events in terms of their perceived outcome!

Figure 6.5 Hero-ape

6.7   The paradigm problem

Science and society inevitably establish whole thought-frames, or **paradigms**, which surround our ways of thinking. The paradigm in which one is reared enables one to see new relationships or truths. Evolutionary thinking has certainly done this for biology, but sometimes a paradigm may also obscure the obvious. Darwin brought a conceptual revolution in scientific thinking into biology, but is it possible that we are unable to see some truths today because of our own paradigm? Early in the twentieth century scientists were convinced that apes developed large brains before they became upright and started to develop any human attributes. It seems they were wrong. Early interpretations pictured australopithecines as blood-thirsty ape-men; it seems now that this was also wrong. Feminists have pointed out that thinking in human evolution has historically been very **male-centred** with its references to 'man'. Another presumption was of a great time distance between our species and the apes, which we now see as probably smaller. Against a background of Darwinian **progressivism** (see section 1.7) and the latter-day racism of our culture, many scientists were unable to see the closeness of all humans as one fully interbreeding and very recent species in which the greatest differences are regional climatic adaptations and cultural differences alone. What misapprehension will be next to fall? Certainly some of the ideas in this book will prove to be wrong and misleading, but at the time of writing the author cannot know which they are! Assumptions which have appeared valid in the past may nevertheless be false.

Questions to think about

1   Given the DNA–DNA hybridisation evidence in chapter 5 suggesting that we are closer to the chimps than the chimps are to the gorillas, would it not make sense to remove the two chimpanzee species from the Gorillinae (see figure 2.1) and classify them with ourselves?

2   Today we recognise five taxonomic kingdoms – Prokaryota, Protoctista, Fungi, Plantae and Animalia. The evolutionist Julian Huxley suggested in 1941 that humans were so different from all other animals that we should be placed in a new (sixth) kingdom of organisms, the 'Psychozoa', to express the quantum leap that humans have made in thought and consciousness. Do you agree? If so, why? If not, why not?

3   What differences between yourself and a small ape might be due largely to reorganising the rate of processes involved in body development?

SEVEN

The apes that stood up

7.1 Two feet rather than four

Among the primates, most animals habitually sit upright and quite a few can stand vertically as well. Although chimps and some monkeys can waddle on two legs, humans are the only primates that are quite erect and frequently on two feet for much of the day. Our **bipedalism**, or upright walking, is not an obvious means of locomotion for a primate. We alone walk with complete steadiness and even run on two legs in a way that is seen nowhere else in the class of mammals. To a baboon our running around would look rather like the behaviour of an ostrich. This chapter explores the development of our first forest ancestors and the emergence of this bipedalism. From the **Palaeocene** (beginning 65 million years ago, or 65 Ma in palaeontological language) to the **Pleistocene** (beginning 2 Ma) there are several hundred fossil primate species known which can be compared to our modern primate cousins. The world's forests were at one time immensely rich with primate species of which only a fraction survive today. Among these fossils we may trace not only their ancestors but also our own.

7.2 The origin of the anthropoids

The Palaeocene forests of Africa, Eurasia and the Americas were extensive, both in millions of years of time and over vast areas of the Earth. The forest environment does not favour fossilisation, and what fossils we have from this environment are often in river sediments, where the remains of other forest animals and the leaves of forest trees and their fruits may also be found. *Plesiadapis* is an abundant fossil from 60 million years ago. This was a long-tailed prosimian not unlike a large grey squirrel in appearance. It was an efficient arboreal leaper. *Necrolemur* is known from the later Eocene; its short face, large orbits for the eyes and hind-limb rigidity indicate a bush-baby type of animal. As yet at this date there were no apes or monkeys. In Egypt, a short distance from Cairo, near the town of Fayum, there are over 200 metres of **Oligocene** sediment deposits exposed. These were laid down between 40 and 25 Ma. This area, now desert, was then part of a huge rainforest lining the banks of the ancient Nile. Significant early primate remains have been found there. Early in the lower sediments is *Apidium*, a small squirrel-like prosimian, which was probably a high canopy dweller not unlike the present monkeys of South America. Later there is *Propliopithecus*, a lightly built form with a tail, but otherwise not unlike a modern gibbon. This early ape has teeth of the anthropoid pattern, with a formula like our own. Contemporary with it is a larger ape, *Aegyptopithecus*. Judging from its teeth this was an arboreal generalised fruit- and leaf-eater. Several complete skulls of this animal are known and it makes a plausible ancestor for the much later **Miocene** apes that were to dominate all of Africa and Eurasia.

7.3   The Miocene apes

The **Miocene** (25 Ma) opens with a period of dense forest environments before the first drying climatic change (see section 4.2 on climate). Two large and plausible ape or gibbon ancestors appear in the fossils from the ancient forests of Africa and Eurasia. These, *Limnopithecus* and *Pliopithecus*, are contemporary with a great radiation of ape-like monkeys. At this time the clear division we make today between apes and monkeys did not exist. It is only after the Miocene that the modern monkeys begin to appear, with baboon-like forms being the most ancient. Among the early Miocene forest apes are numerous forms generally known as **dryopithecines**. *Dryopithecus* itself seems to have first lived in Africa and later spread to Asia and Europe. At this time the gibbons may have begun their separate ancestry from the great apes. Although initially found in Africa, gibbons are now only known in modern South East Asia. The early dryopithecines were apes with thin tooth enamel and large canines, not unlike modern chimpanzees. The genus *Dryopithecus* includes that once termed *Proconsul*. There were at least six species of *Dryopithecus* in Africa, Europe and Asia, during the Miocene period. Two of the African species, *D. nyanzae* and *D. major* (dating from 20 Ma), are, respectively, so like the modern chimpanzee and the gorilla that they make plausible modern ape ancestors, although it might well be that the African apes are more recently related to each other and to ourselves, rather than being separate from this very ancient date. There are enough ape fossils to say that these early hominoids were **sexually dimorphic**, the males weighing 60 kg and the females only about 30 kg. The males, judging from the fossils, had large canines and they were probably therefore, like modern baboons, polygynous, with a single dominant male in the troop fathering the majority of the offspring.

In the mid-Miocene there was a clear shift in climate. At least some of the forests at that time became drier and gave place to more open woodland. It seems that some of these early apes ventured into drier savannahs and may possibly have been the first to feed on a harder non-soft-fruit diet in these more open environments. *Kenyapithecus* was one such early East

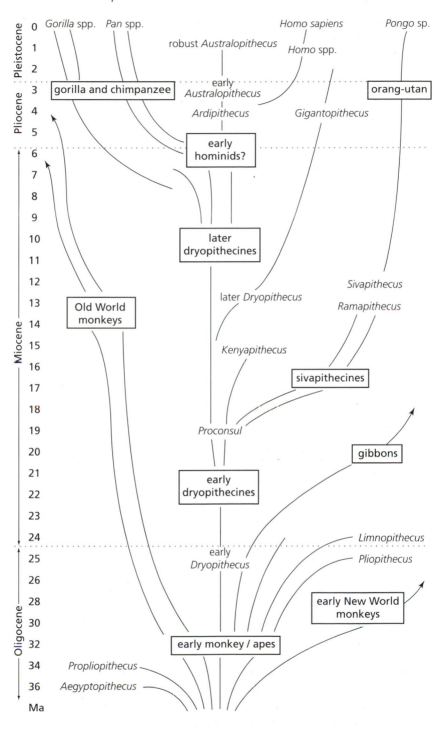

Figure 7.1   The phylogenetic bush of fossil anthropoids (see also figure 5.4)

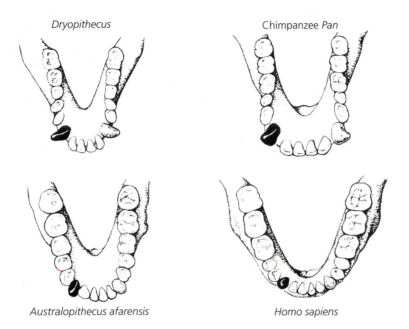

Dryopithecus   Chimpanzee *Pan*

Australopithecus afarensis   *Homo sapiens*

Figure 7.2 Jaw shapes and relative tooth sizes of hominoids (not to scale). The jaw of the chimpanzee is more robust than that of the early dryopithecine; by contrast, the australopithecine molars are larger and the canines and incisors smaller. Humans follow this size-reducing trend.

African ape with thick tooth enamel. The **sivapithecine group** were apes that had this thick enamel adaptation and differed in details of their palate and facial structure. If they had their origins in Africa, like the dryopithecines (see figure 7.1), they too spread out of the continent, but there is absolutely no evidence that they were effective bipeds. Virtually no skeletal remains are known. *Sivapithecus* (named in honour of the Hindu god Siva) was first discovered in Pakistan in 1915. *Ramapithecus* is another sivapithecine convergent with *Kenyapithecus*. *Ramapithecus* had very low canines of a type that is to be found later in the fossil record in the man-ape australopithecines (see chapter 8). It was this similarity that caused *Ramapithecus* to be classed, for 20 years, as the strongest contender to be an early hominid. The modern orang-utan is from a sivapithecine line, though today it is an ape of the densest forest and is not at all adapted to open woodland. The more conservative forest dryopithecines gave rise to a second wave of woodland- and savannah-adapted invaders, in the form of the **australopithecines**, in the following **Pliocene** era (5–2 Ma). We may therefore see the modern great apes of Africa as **relict apes** in a forest environment at equilibrium, that may have changed little in millions of years.

In Pliocene Europe the dryopithecines had died out. Perhaps they could not cope with the colder climate, more marked seasons or competing or aggressive bears (a group of carnivores that have never entered Africa). In

Asia, however, two ancient large herbivorous species of ground ape did linger on from the Miocene to the Pliocene and on into the Pleistocene in a niche possibly comparable to that of the African robust australopithecines (see chapter 8). These were species of *Gigantopithecus*, a huge ground ape comparable in size to the African gorilla. These might have held their own against bears and lions as witnessed by their massive teeth and jaws. Their fossil 'dragon teeth' are known in Chinese folk medicine. This giant ape may have become extinct only in relatively recent human times. Some people see their folk-memory in the mythical tales of the Himalayan 'yeti' or even as the North American 'big-foot'!

7.4   The origin of bipedalism

The Miocene became drier towards its end (5 Ma) and this drying of the climates of Africa continued into the Pliocene. This is a key period in human evolutionary history and to date we only have good fossils from about 4.5 Ma or later. When all the fossil evidence and molecular evidence is considered together, it is now thought likely that the origins of the drier woodland apes' adaptations that we find at 4 Ma may have begun at any time between 10 and 5 Ma. Probably we are looking at the period of 9–7 Ma as the first faltering footsteps to bipedalism. More certainly, by 3.6 Ma we find hominid footprints that could only have been made by a greatly modified animal.

What prompted the change from quadrupedalism to bipedalism? What advantages are there in bipedal walking and what disadvantages? The answers to such questions involve hypothesis making followed by experimental testing of the resulting predictions. Before looking at these hypotheses, it is important to understand our modern human locomotor and skeletal adaptation.

7.5   Balancing upright

Upright walking on two legs rather than four involves a change in the centre of gravity of the body, from above and between the four legs to above and between the two (see figure 7.3). In a standing human, the centre of gravity is in the pelvic region and acts downwards just behind a line between the hip joints and in front of a line between the knee joints. As the femur is flexed forwards in movement and the tibia is flexed back, it will be clear that in standing upright on two legs a position is achieved whereby the hip and knee joints are locked in full extension. This standing position we know as restful and it requires little muscular effort to hold it. Again, if we squat with our trunk fully upright but the hip and knee joints fully bent at an acute angle to the body, the centre of gravity still passes downwards between our feet. These **bipedal positions** free our hands.

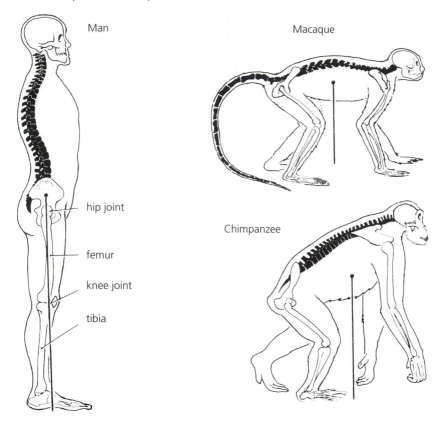

Figure 7.3 Bipedal and quadrupedal stances. In the quadrupedal macaque (*Cercopithecus*) the vertebral column is arched between pelvic and pectoral cantilever supports. In the more upright but still quadrupedal chimpanzee (*Pan*) the column is straighter. In humans the vertebral column has reverse curvatures in the lumbar and cervical regions which bring the trunk and head above the centre of gravity.

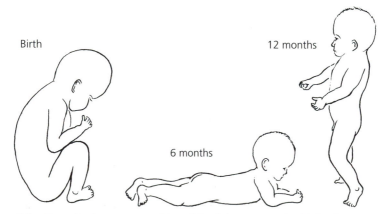

Figure 7.4 Growth changes to achieve bipedal posture. At birth the vertebral column is 'C'-shaped. Neck retroflexion develops from two months onwards while the lumbar secondary curvature develops when the infant learns to walk.

In bipedal standing, the weight of the trunk and upper parts of the body is almost all carried by the vertebral column acting down on the **sacroiliac** of the lower back, whereas quadrupedal animals have an arched bridge-like structure between forelimbs and hind limbs counterpoised by the cantilevered weight of rump and head. Although a human infant is born with such a single-curved back, as the child grows the neck develops a secondary **retroflexion** and then the small of the back hollows as we learn to stand erect (see figure 7.4). Leaning over forwards is always hard on the back muscles. Whether we stand, walk or even run upright, the weight of our body is transmitted down this **balanced spinal column** to the sacroiliac and pelvic support of the femur heads, long bones and knees.

7.6 Walking and running

We have seen that in humans the **knees** are close together beneath the centre of gravity. This means that when walking we are less likely to waddle from side to side as a seemingly bow-legged chimpanzee does (try a knees-apart chimp-walk imitation and you will see how much hard work it is). Our femur has a long and angled neck and our knee joint is not at right angles to the femur shaft. This **valgus angle** of the knee is diagnostic of a bipedal hominid (see figure 7.5). Despite this bringing of the knees under the centre of gravity, when one leg is lifted off the ground in walking there is tendency for the pelvis to drop down on the same side. This is countered by the contraction of **abductor muscles**, the gluteus medius and minor (see figure 7.5), which run from the ilium (hip bone) to the top of the femur shaft. These abductor muscles contract on each side alternately as one walks to minimise

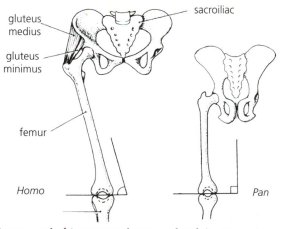

Figure 7.5 Human and chimpanzee femur and pelvic comparison. The gluteus muscles of the hip lift the pelvis up so preventing tilting when the opposite leg is off the ground. Note that in humans, unlike apes, the knee joint is not at right angles to the femur shaft.

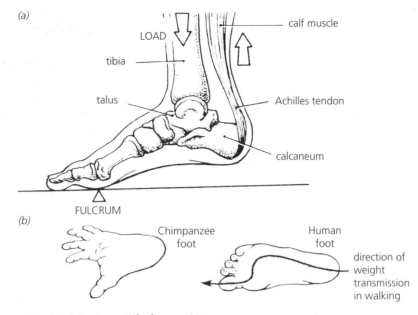

(a)

Figure 7.6 Modifications of the human foot

pelvic tilting. The contraction occurs on the side on which you are using your leg for standing. This lifts your pelvis on the other side and allows the leg to swing through as you walk or run.

As one starts to walk or run one leans forward. You will fall if you do not move your legs forward and support the new position of your centre of gravity. Once 'up and running' the body is carried vertically, but the trunk is thrown back behind the pelvis as you decelerate and come again to a halt, standing with your centre of gravity above your knees.

The human **foot and ankle** are also greatly modified (see figure 7.6). Compared to an ape, the human ankle joint is fairly rigid and will not rotate easily left or right, but may be pointed down well. There is a large heel bone (calcaneum) to which a well-developed Achilles tendon is attached, being the insertion of the soleus and gastrocnemius (calf muscles) and providing a powerful means of extending the foot. If extension takes place during a stride, it will not be a flat-footed step, but will provide a propulsive lifting force at each step. The whole structure of the human foot is modified for this extra propulsive effort. The apes have an unvaulted foot structure and an opposable big toe (hallux). The human big toe is barely opposable and is aligned parallel to the others. The metatarsals (foot bones) are elongated, vaulted and aligned in parallel. As we walk there is a curved line of weight transmission from the heel along the outer edge of the foot to the ball of the big toe (look at some wet footprints on a bathroom floor). These modifications are considerable and must have taken many millions of years to perfect. They were essentially complete 2 million years ago and, judging from the fossil Laetoli footprints, well under way 2 million years before that.

7.7   Advantages and disadvantages of bipedalism

Because a chimpanzee on all fours can outrun a human, it is tempting to see bipedalism as inefficient and slow. Why did it evolve? This question is generally placed in the ecological context of climatic change. When forests become drier there is a vegetative succession to savannah woodland of a more open kind. The proto-hominids of Africa should perhaps be seen as very lightweight apes compared to modern quadrupedal chimps. The bonobo or pigmy chimpanzee, which is arguably closer to us genetically, is a smaller and more upright animal than its more quadrupedal cousin. Young bonobos and, indeed, gibbons demonstrate much more verticality from their arboreal swinging behaviour. Might the earliest hominids have been more upright naturally than modern chimps? Some upright walking is found in all of the apes. Unsurprisingly, chimpanzees in open woodland spend much more time on the ground than they do in more wooded environments. In such situations chimps tend to stand or move more upright, particularly when greeting each other, fighting, wading through streams, looking out for predators or opponents, carrying objects such as sticks, gathering food or carrying infants under one arm. Each of these **ideas supporting bipedalism** may be explored as a plausible hypothetical avenue that would encourage greater bipedalism.

There is one fossil record difficulty, however, that needs to be addressed in this discussion. At 4 Ma the earliest australopithecines are not at all associated with open savannah but with quite closed woodland. This suggests that some walking was well developed before the proto-hominids left the forest. Bioenergetic studies have shown that although bipedal running is an expensive way of moving for the amount of energy expended, bipedal walking is significantly less energy-demanding as a sustained method of slow locomotion than quadrupedal walking in apes. Perhaps if there was a severe food shortage in a drought, or fruiting trees were scarce and long distances apart, upright walking was favoured as a more energy-efficient way of travelling. A thermoregulatory argument has been advanced to suggest that by upright walking in the tropical sun the early hominids would have got less hot, with the sun only on their heads, and not on their backs! Certainly, these animals would not initially have been safe from predatory cats and hyenas if far from the trees. As our earliest ape ancestors moved out of the forest, how fast they could run to find and get up a tree, whilst carrying their infants or sticks for self-defence, might well have been a major factor in their survival. We may never know exactly.

The **Laetoli footprints** (3.6 Ma) are one of the most remarkable fossil discoveries (see figure 7.7), showing an almost modern stride. A study of the footprint bed reveals that after a fresh volcanic carbonatite lava ash fall, an adult and two younger individuals walked across an open stretch of dry lake flats. Shortly after, rain turned the cement-like ash to solid rock for per-

Figure 7.7 Laetoli footprints. Three early hominids walked upright and left these footprints 3.5 million years ago.

petuity. Analysis of the stride length indicates an adult height of four or five feet. The smallest child's prints are right beside those of the adult and keeping step as if they were holding hands. The older child's steps follow behind those of the adult, each foot placed in the larger print impressions. Crossing the hominid trail are the prints of an extinct miniature horse, *Hipparion*.

Questions to think about

1 What is the difference between a primate, an anthropoid, a hominoid and a hominid? Give an example of each and say when each taxon first evolved.

2 With reference to your own skeletal bones, muscles and joints, can you describe exactly how you walk two strides?

3 List all the advantages and disadvantages of bipedalism for a very early hominid in an open woodland.

EIGHT

The australopithecines:
the man-apes of Africa

8.1   The first man-apes

An ape that walks upright like us is described as a **hominid** but its nature
certainly need not be human. When comparing an early hominid with a
modern chimp such a bipedal modification might be its only additional
human attribute. The semantic difference between an **ape-man** and a **man-
ape** is perhaps too fine to argue in depth, but the term 'ape-man' raises
mental images that are likely to mislead. To describe australopithecines,
then, as 'man-apes' perhaps only dodges the stereotype, but it does also add
emphasis to the word ape – these were apes with human skeletal characteristics and not brutish and hairy men.

Our understanding of the extinct australopithecines has been greatly
influenced by the sequence and circumstances of their discovery and by the
personalities and opinions that have prevailed since the 1920s.
Palaeoanthropologists agree that these man-apes first appeared at least 4.5
million years ago. They were adapted to light woodland or savannah living
and, so far as we know, were only found in the continent of Africa. They had
an apparently herbivorous dentition but, when compared to modern apes,
had relatively reduced canines and incisors and slightly thicker enamel. Some
had immense food-crushing molar teeth. They were almost fully bipedal but
probably retained an acrobatic nimbleness in tree climbing in comparison
with ourselves. Many were very small, some little more than a metre in adult
height, and very strong for their size. Several australopithecine species
adapted increasingly in the direction of a more massive size and in
consuming a bulk vegetable diet. In all probability it was some early australopithecine that gave rise anagenetically to *Homo*. What is not debated is that, of
the diversity of man-apes which did evolve, all are now extinct.

8.2   The discovery of the earliest African hominids

In 1912 the forger of 'Piltdown man' (now alleged to be Martin A. C. Hinton)
played, no doubt unconsciously, on the popular ape-man image. The
Piltdown forgery (see footnote to section 4.6) was compounded of a full-
sized human cranium and an orang-utan jaw. It was a cleverly devised hoax.

But this early twentieth-century notion of the 'missing link' with its big brain and heavy jaw prevented palaeontologists from recognising the australopithecines for what we now see them to be. Most were quite dismissive of a very small-brained ape fossil discovered in South Africa in 1924. **Raymond Dart** obtained what is now called the **Taung baby** (see figure 8.1) from a limestone quarry near Johannesburg, where he was then a young lecturer in anatomy at Witwatersrand University. It consisted of a limestone cast of the cranial interior (or endocranial cast) and a complete face and lower jaw. He recognised that its cranial volume, though small, was larger in relative terms than that of an ape, and that the teeth were of human type. Most importantly, the **foramen magnum**, the opening at the back of the skull through which the spinal cord emerges, was below the brain case and not positioned further back as in the apes. With some excitement he published an account of his upright 'southern ape' and named it *Australopithecus africanus*, suggesting a position for it intermediate between apes and humans.

In the 1930s **Robert Broom**, a well-known South African palaeontologist and a colleague of Dart's, took up the trail and became convinced that other early men might be found in the continent. He made his first discovery of a larger-skulled adult australopithecine at **Sterkfontein**. This site, like two more he discovered at **Kromdraai** and **Swartkrans**, were vertical fissure limestone caves that had been filled in from the top. The fossils were well preserved though they were almost concretely fast in the rock. Dart returned to fossil hunting in 1947 at a fifth limestone cave site at **Makapansgat**. Here he unearthed very many fragmentary australopithecine fossils, largely the crushed remains of what we now know to be leopard prey and hyena scavenging. At the time, however, Dart attributed (we now believe mistakenly) carnivorous and cannibal tendencies to his little apes. We now realise that all these man-apes found gathered in the limestone caves may well have been the remains of leopard kills. Leopards are still the principal predators of African woodland. Indeed one skull bears the unmistakable marks of canine teeth, indicating exactly how such a small ape may have been dragged by a leopard to its tree larder. Broom and Dart gave a whole constellation of names to their new finds. Today we see them as falling either into the more slender, lightly built **gracile** form of australopithecine or the more heavily built **robust** species.

By the late 1950s, with Piltdown discredited, few doubted that Africa sustained more hope of yielding good fossils of early man than anywhere else. In Kenya, the archaeologist **Louis Leakey** was increasingly turning his attention to fossil hunting. He had already made considerable advances in the knowledge of African prehistory. A deep series of sediments at **Olduvai** in northern Tanzania had attracted his particular interest for it was extraordinarily rich in fossils. Here Louis and his wife **Mary Leakey** made the discovery in 1959 of the most perfect hominid skull yet to be found. Seized by that feeling of uniqueness and pride in one's discovery that is the palaeontologist's chief reward, they gave the fossil a new genus name,

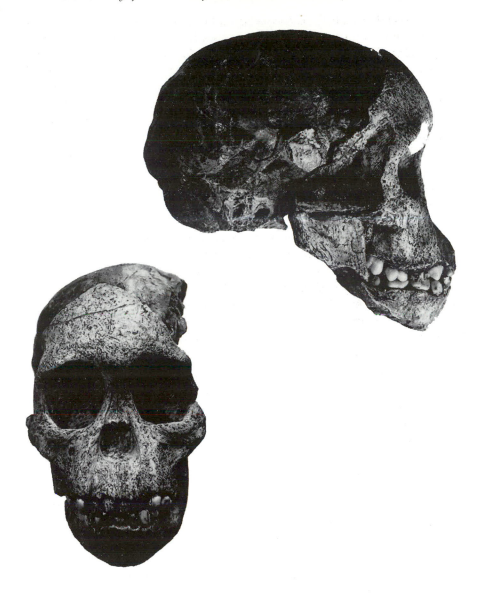

Figure 8.1 The Taung baby. The first fossil hominid discovery in Africa is the type specimen of the genus *Australopithecus*. The limestone filling of the cranium has formed a natural endocast to show the former brain size. The relatively large brain size for the facial size of this 5-year-old gives the infant a more human appearance than an adult would have.

Zinjanthropus or 'Nutcracker man', after the prodigious molars of this robust australopithecine fossil.

The late twentieth century has seen a huge acceleration of exploration and discovery. The missing pieces of the jigsaw puzzle have poured in almost faster than they can be put together. Louis and Mary's son **Richard Leakey** and (principally) his wife **Maeve Leakey** and **Alan Walker** have worked Kenyan fossil sites at **Koobi Fora** on the shore of **Lake Turkana** and in the region of the great **Omo** River that drains south into that lake from the Ethiopian highlands. The Koobi Fora sediments span a period going back to 3 Ma, and a diversity of human and australopithecine forms are now known. Even earlier sediments which overlap Koobi Fora and Omo in time are found at **Laetoli**, in Tanzania, and at **Hadar**, in Ethiopia. Here the most recent significant collections have been made and the most ancient australopithecines of all discovered. The sites discovered over 20 years ago in Ethiopia by **Don Johanson** and **Tim White** are perhaps the most important (see figure 4.1). Today we have hundreds of specimens.

8.3   The early *Australopithecus* species

Despite all the discoveries the early hominid story is still in limbo between 4.5 and 8 million years ago. This fossil gap is a 'black hole' – no light has yet come out of it to illuminate the early story. The geological record indicates a shrinking of the extensive tropical forest at 5 Ma in favour of seasonally drier woodlands. Here the first man-apes appear on the scene as different from the apes. The extremely fragmentary fossils that exist are of small unspecialised ape-like forms comparable *in size* to a modern chimpanzee. There are presently recognised three arguably different and perhaps successive early East African species spanning 1.5 million years before the later robust australopithecines appear.

Ardipithecus (Australopithecus) ramidus

This is currently the oldest known arguably hominid form. In 1994 at **Aramis** in Ethiopia, at a site dated at 4.4 Ma, Tim White's team found isolated teeth, cranial fragments and arm bones of a small ape showing in its teeth and skull some clear affinity to later hominids. It is hard to say from the evidence if these were already bipedal forms, but the many other fossils from these sites are certainly from woodland and not savannah animals. Tim White, their discoverer, places this fossil form in a new genus *Ardipithecus*.

Australopithecus anamensis

This is the most recently discovered new hominid. In 1995 at Omo in Kenya, at a site dated at 4.1 Ma, Maeve Leakey's team found sufficient remains to identify a form with clear bipedalism, some primitive ape-like features and others more like those of early *Homo*. One of the great excitements of fossil hunting is that more fossils of our earliest human ancestors are undoubtedly waiting to be unearthed.

Australopithecus afarensis

In the mid 1970s Don Johanson and Tim White discovered what are still the best known early australopithecine remains at Hadar in Ethiopia. *Australopithecus afarensis* is typified by the fossil **Lucy** (AL 288-1; see figure 8.2). Discovered in 1974, this almost complete fossil individual was immediately seen to be a hominid, since the knee and pelvis were of a characteristically human form, and from the width of the pelvis was probably female. Lucy obtained her name from the Beatles' song 'Lucy in the Sky with Diamonds', which was being played in the camp on the night of her fortuitous discovery. Other more fragmented specimens, from some 13 individuals of mixed ages that may have been drowned together in a gully flash flood, are of the same species. Fragmentary tooth and jaw remains discovered by Mary Leakey at Laetoli in Tanzania belong to the same species. In

Figure 8.2 Lucy: a reconstruction of *Australopithecus afarensis*

view of the fully bipedal adaptation of Lucy's pelvis, femur head and angled knees, there seems no reason to doubt that this species was responsible for the exactly contemporary Laetoli footprints. The fossils of this earliest form, dating from 4.0 Ma, are now as well known as the later australopithecines.

Contemporary bedded fossils indicate that these earliest australopithecines were woodland or tree-covered-savannah dwellers. They varied in height, as adults, from 1–1.5 m, but were thick-boned and of muscular build, weighing from 30–70 kg. Thus, despite only having the stature of present-day primary school children, they would have been formidably tough and agile. From the femur shape there is no doubt that they walked bipedally, but the pelvis is not of fully human form. Their gait was more rolling than our own, the stabilising power of the lesser gluteal muscles being underdeveloped (see figure 7.5). The Laetoli footprints show an already arched foot suggesting some propulsive foot extension, but the foot was not like ours in that there was still a divergent big toe (see figure 7.6). Given the greater arm length to leg length ratio than in modern humans, obvious hip and shoulder mobility and evidence of considerably ape-like wrist bones and more curled fingers, one must conclude that they were also still very much at home in the trees. On our scale these animals were child-sized. Modern human children have better shoulder anatomy for brachiating than adults. You only have to look at the tree-climbing ease and acrobatic skill of small children to realise that their parents have literally outgrown the arboreal habit. Early australopithecines should be viewed as creatures for whom trees were probably important, as a refuge from predators as well as sources of picked plant food. The image of a very human (albeit diminutive) body is clear, but the skulls are remarkably ape-like in this early form.

The *A. afarensis* range of cranial volumes (a reasonable equivalent to brain size) is 380–450 cm^3; that for chimpanzees is 300–400 cm^3. This is certainly nowhere near the 1345 cm^3 mean for modern man. Their jaws were smaller than a chimp's but larger than the later gracile australopithecines, with flattened teeth adapted for extensive chewing of food (see figure 8.3). We may tentatively guess that their diet was more refined than that of a chimp. This suggests some use of tools such as digging sticks and stones to find and process such foods as plant tubers and nuts. There is evidence that canine reduction from ape-like form was recent, for in some jaws, probably those of males, the canines are modest, somewhat pointed and protruding from the tooth row, but worn flat at the tips. This may reflect a change in social structure (big canines amongst primates are associated with troops where single males have a large harem of females) or with a change in diet. The wielding of clubs as weapons might substitute for the defensive function of large canines. To our human view of a face, they were **prognathous**, with forward-jutting jaws and lips, in marked contrast to their low-crowned heads, flattened faces with little nose and no chin protruding below. Figure 8.2 is based upon a reconstruction of the facial features of *Australopithecus afarensis* by the anatomical artist Jay Matternes.

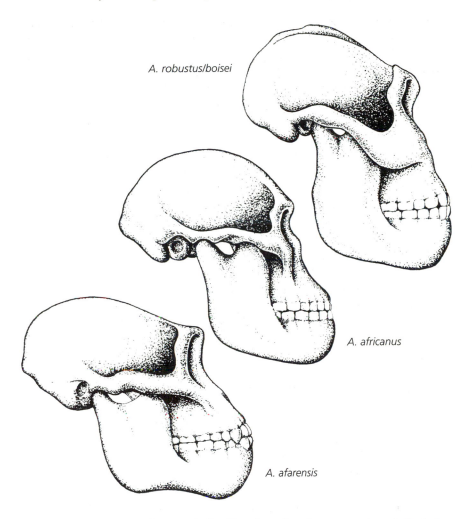

A. robustus/boisei

A. africanus

A. afarensis

Figure 8.3 Australopithecine skulls. The three best-known species of *Australo-pithecus* may be separated in time to some extent. The largest, *Australopithecus robustus/boisei*, is the most specialised of the man-apes, being adapted for the mighty chewing of a vegetable diet. Only the early australopithecines are close to the human line (see figure 8.4).

Australopithecus afarensis is absent from the top horizons of Hadar at around 2.8 Ma. Before this time there was a considerable radiation of the primitive hominid stock. By 2.5 Ma some larger-brained but still big-toothed hominids had evolved. Such undoubted human ancestors must be placed in the genus *Homo*. These earliest true humans are described in the next chapter. Contemporary with them were other hominids derived also from the stem australopithecines. These later man-apes are broadly divisible into a continuation of the lightly built **'gracile'** forms and, later throughout South and Eastern Africa, more heavily built **'robust'** forms.

8.4   The gracile *Australopithecus africanus*

In South Africa there was a lightly built australopithecine dating from between 2.7 and 2.2 million years ago. Those specimens that are relatively small-brained, compared to *Homo*, and not massively molared are ascribed to *Australopithecus africanus*, represented by the Taung baby and by specimens from Sterkfontein. Ecologically these were still woodland dwellers. They differed from the earlier 'Lucy' type (*A. afarensis*) in being of generally larger size and were noticeably bigger-brained, but still very heavy-jawed. Cranial capacities range from 375–575 cm³ with a mean of 450 cm³. We know little of their way of life. The complete pelvic bones from Sterkfontein indicate a fully upright posture. There is no firm association between this species and early stone tools, and that any hunting or scavenged-meat eating was adopted is supposition alone. *Australopithecus africanus* fits well onto a line of phyletic descent from the earliest australo-pithecines, but it fits less well as an antecedent of some of the robust forms that were to appear later. 2.5 million years ago there were probably clusters of hominids with diverging dietary specialisms besides other, geographical divergences. With certainty, one of these lines led to ourselves (see figure 8.4).

8.5   The robust australopithecines

In South and East Africa, the robust australopithecines, represented first by Broom's and Louis Leakey's specimens, have long been problematic but now clearly appear to be a side issue so far as human evolution is concerned. This clade (branch) of man-apes is distinctive for 1.5 million years before their extinction. Absolute dating of the Swartkrans remains is impossible because of the lack of volcanic rock for potassium–argon dating, but what is significant is that the fauna associated with these fossils is more modern while that at the other *A. africanus* sites in South Africa is clearly older. Robustness followed gracility. This interpretation is fully borne out in East Africa, where one more robust form with clear links to Lucy has been described as *Australopithecus aethiopicus*. In 1985 the cranium of a highly distinctive and very early robust form was found in **West Turkana** by Alan Walker. Nicknamed 'the black skull' from its colour, this dish-faced prog-nathous form is linked with several other early robust remains. Later East African forms are more vertically faced and certainly more massively built. These are classified as *Australopithecus boisei*, retaining Louis Leakey's original species name for the 'Olduvai nutcracker man' (*Zinjanthropus boisei* – see section 8.2) but reassigning it to the *Australopithecus* genus. The later robusts are radiometrically dated between about 2 and 1 Ma. *A. boisei* is either regarded as a different geographical race or as a separate species from the South African *Australopithecus robustus*. We are thus obliged to see

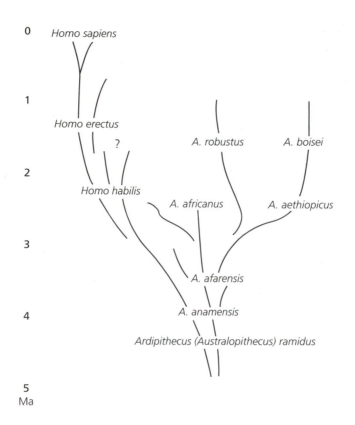

Figure 8.4 The hominid bush

these massive-molared man-apes as a late offshoot of the early australo-pithecines. They became extinct within the last million years in Africa.

The distinctive features of all these robust australopithecines are their greater overall size and the extensive modification of skull and jaw features for mighty chewing. In the largest forms the incisors and canines are much reduced and the molars greatly enlarged and flattened. The jaw is deep and strongly buttressed with bone, while the rather flat cranium has a median sagittal crest of bone, as in the gorilla, to which massive temporal muscles would have attached. These features all suggest that this larger australo-pithecine, standing fully 5 feet (1.5 m) high and weighing quite as much as a modern human, spent much of its time chewing a hard vegetable diet. Study of the enamel thickness and surface microwear show no scratches that could be associated with a diet containing soil particles or bone. This seems to rule out meat, root and even herb-leaf eating. The thick enamel would have protected the tooth from cracking if very small hard seeds were present. By contrast, some South African *robustus* teeth have a microwear that is very pitted by soil scratching, indicating a diet of roots and tubers. As in the modern gorilla, such bulk eating is a solution if this low-energy and low-protein vegetarian diet was to sustain such a large non-ruminant.

At Koobi Fora robust australopithecines are **sexually dimorphic**, being in two size classes with larger males and smaller females. We should expect there to be some genetic, sex-governed size and proportion differences. The brain size of the robust species is in the range 410–600 cm^3 with a mean of 504 cm^3. For their size they were not necessarily more intelligent than the other australopithecines, indeed such a brain volume is comparable to that of the gorilla. Size and scaling considerations provide one of the best reasons for thinking that these latter-day man-apes were merely larger versions of the earlier australopithecines. Such **allometry** (change in proportion with growth change in size) cannot however explain the sudden brain volume increases that occurred in the rise of the genus *Homo*. As we shall see in the next two chapters, humans evolved side by side with these now vanished man-apes who dwindle from the fossil record in the mid-Pleistocene. Our more human ancestors may well have driven these man-apes to eventual extinction.

Questions to think about

1 What features of the *Australopithecus africanus* 'Taung baby' (see figure 8.1) caused Raymond Dart to consider it on the line of human ancestry?

2 What criteria could you use to decide whether a fossil australo-pithecine was mentally more advanced than a chimpanzee?

3 If we discovered a relict population of australopithecines today, should we conserve them in their natural habitat, try to civilise them or put them in a zoo?

NINE

Homo habilis: *the making of humankind*

9.1 Hominisation

Homo habilis crosses the threshold from man-apes to humans. Besides fulfilling the traditional archaeological criterion for inclusion in the genus *Homo*, the making of tools, this species clearly demonstrates the expansion of brain size that allows the development of characteristically human intellectual, linguistic and social attributes and finer manipulative skills. This process of becoming human in a biological and social sense is often called **hominisation**. It will have become clear to the reader that other primates hint at human nature, but there was a threshold point in evolution, reached 2–3 million years ago, when development towards humankind had an auto-catalytic effect that seems to have accelerated the hominising process. This chapter is also concerned with the **hypothesis making** that is an essential background for the testing of predictions.

9.2 Manipulative skills

Hands, the characteristically modified forelimbs of primates, differ from paws in having **prehensility**, the ability to grasp objects in one hand, and **opposability**, whereby the thumb can grip against the other digits and hold on to a small object. The degree to which the hands of primates are strongly prehensile or finely opposable varies greatly, but it is in humans alone that the hand is most fully modified and most dextrously controlled. The most significant anatomical adaptation, distinguishing the human hand from that of an ape, is firstly a highly mobile thumb joint which has a basal saddle-shaped rocking articulation. Secondly, the terminal thumb bone, bearing the nail, is relatively elongated and broadened to support the pad at the end of the digit. Apes have hands that are largely adapted for locomotion rather than for fine manipulation. For example, the gibbon has a very small thumb that does not interfere with the brachiating hooking grasp of their elongated fingers. The gorilla has a much-curled hand with solid sole-like knuckles (see figure 9.1). The great apes appear clumsy by our standards of dexterity and, although skilled by animal standards, give the impression that great concentration and effort are needed to manipulate any fine object.

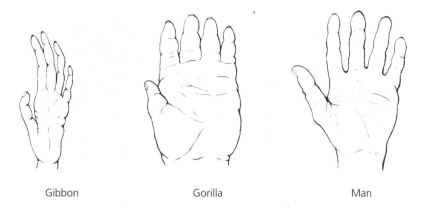

| Gibbon | Gorilla | Man |

Figure 9.1   The hands of primates

Humans have two types of grip, a prehensile **power grip** for actions requiring the application of strength and a **precision grip** in which the thumb pad opposes the tips of the other digits. Thus we apply a power grip to a tennis racket and a precision grip to a pen. Our finely controlled individual finger and hand movements are a product of very considerable motor cortical development in the association areas of the brain. The spinal cord in early *Homo* was considerably smaller than our own, perhaps indicating less fine nervous control.

The species name *habilis*, meaning 'handy' or 'dextrous', was given by Louis Leakey in 1964 to the hominid remains associated with the earliest tools at **Olduvai**. The fingers of *Homo habilis* were only slightly in-curved and the thumb only a little shorter than ours (with a shorter terminal phalanx). With a smaller brain, nervous control may have limited the hand's usefulness somewhat, but the earliest stone tools could have been made without difficulty using a power grip alone. The relationship between hand and brain lies behind the development of the most primitive technologies. Although earlier hominids were undoubtedly tool users, perhaps using sticks as chimpanzees do, and may have modified them for use, early humans are the first makers of tool kits of selected and worked implements. Finding fashioned **stone tools** tells us something of the intentions in the mind of their maker. The earliest chipped cobblestones are from **Hadar** in Ethiopia and date from 2.6 Ma.

9.3   Language and speech

Apes do not talk, but some people never seem to cease from this peculiarly human activity. **Speech** is only one form of meaningful communication. Although speech is exclusively human, apes certainly have the rudiments of language. Apes may sign and signal effectively in ways we yet do not under-

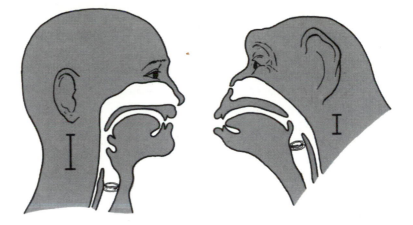

Figure 9.2 The human and ape vocal apparatus. Compared to the ape, humans have a much larger vocal chamber with a greater capacity for voice modification. It is believed that apes are unable to communicate by speech sounds, not because of these deficiencies alone, but also because they lack the brain control required for using the throat muscles involved in sound production.

stand: they grimace, gesticulate and hoot to communicate with each other. However, they seem to have no syntactic language in which symbols with meaning are consecutively ordered to convey sustained transmissions of information.

Experiments with chimpanzees show that they can certainly follow some human speech in the sense of hearing the different sounds, linking sound sequences and associating them with meaning. Kanzi, a bonobo (pygmy chimp or *Pan paniscus*) reared by Sue Savage-Rumbaugh, is well able to follow her spoken instructions. On walks through the woods Kanzi can go and gather specific fruits or objects which Sue asks him to collect and he follows her simple spoken instructions as an infant child might do. However, Kanzi has never spoken or even tried to speak. The reason for this is partly that apes have a very short pharynx between the mouth or buccal cavity and vocal cords of the larynx, their palate is flattened and the tongue shallow-rooted. This makes some vowel and many consonantal sounds impossible to form. Very young human infants have an ape-like laryngeal anatomy and are therefore anatomically unable to speak. But as we grow up, perhaps due in part to our upright stance and retracted face, the pharynx deepens, the palate arches and the tongue becomes more deep-rooted to form the anterior wall of the vocal chamber. With better tongue and lip control and this muscular throat chamber, we have a greater capacity for vocal modification in the production of sound. Can such anatomical differences alone account for the apes' incapacity to learn vocal speech control, or could they also be deficient in brain control?

In order to puzzle this out, many studies have been done on ape intelligence and language-learning. Chimpanzees are undoubtedly extremely intelligent animals, using their ample aptitude for learning to cope with complex social situations and no doubt also, in the wild, to find and remember the numerous geographical localities of their home range. Recent studies of bonobos in the wild strongly suggest that they may signal to each other using flattened and broken vegetation to indicate where they have gone in the forest. Socially they are sophisticated and as individuals manifest a degree of awareness of themselves that better enables them to interact with other individuals. They are 'self' conscious, for they undoubtedly do recognise *themselves* as themselves in a mirror, or on a video-recording, something that other mammals apparently do not. They can tell a live video image of themselves from a recorded one. Of the many attempts that have been made to teach apes **language**, only those involving signing with the fingers and with particular signed words, such as American Sign Language (ASL), or those employing visual object word symbols such as differently coloured plastic tokens, have had much success. Using such signs and symbols a chimp may easily learn a vocabulary of over one hundred words. Koko, a gorilla reared and trained in ASL by Penny Patterson, used over 300 signs regularly out of some 600 learned altogether, but although able to joke, swear, tease her trainer and even invent new words (like 'white-tiger' for a zebra), she was limited in her capacity to invent the elaborate representational expressions that lie at the base of human language. It thus seems that we can communicate with apes as we would with a two-year-old human infant. However, it may well be that humans have not learned ape communication signals sufficiently to appreciate the languages that they are using with each other.

Many apes use their right hand more than the left, especially – as in humans – for finer manipulative movements. Fine control of the right hand is governed by the left hemisphere of the brain. Speech centres are close to these fine manipulation centres and it might be that the former have developed in humans close to original brain areas used for delicate grooming operations (a form of social communication) and perhaps signing communication. Two general areas of the human brain apparently work together to make human speech and language possible. They are named after two neuroanatomists and are called Broca's and Wernicke's areas. **Broca's area** in the left frontal lobe is concerned with grammatical word form and sequence, that is syntax, and acts as the co-ordinating centre that instructs the motor cortical areas, just posterior to it, which control the lips, tongue and larynx. **Wernicke's area** is in the left temporal lobe and is the major centre for storage of auditory, visual and verbal (hence also heard and read) memory. Wernicke's area is thus the 'word bank' and Broca's area the 'synthesiser' acting under the higher centres of the brain. It should be noted that this activity is localised in the left hemisphere almost exclusively. Such lateralised specialisation is thought to be more a brain feature of humans and there is less evidence of it in apes. Traces of the early evolutionary development of these specialised brain areas are intriguingly revealed on the

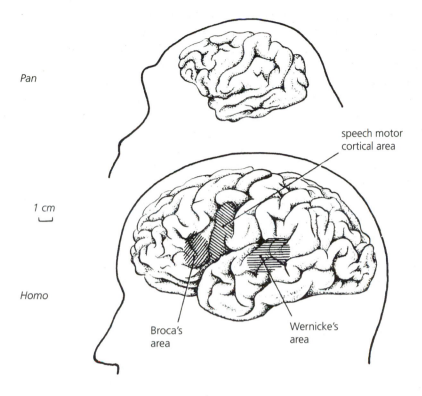

Pan

speech motor
cortical area

1 cm

Homo

Broca's
area

Wernicke's
area

Figure 9.3   A comparison of ape and human brains

inner surfaces of fossil crania, for during life the outer brain membranes and blood vessels that closely follow the brain's convoluted contours become imprinted in the surrounding cranial bone. Endocasts of hominid crania have been minutely studied by many researchers, revealing that the left hemisphere frontal, parietal and temporal lobes of *Homo habilis* and *Homo erectus* have these speech centre enlargements to a greater extent than either the modern apes or the endocasts of early and robust australopithecines. This is the only real clue we have that early hominids may have begun not just speech but also the exchange of ideas and information.

9.4   Changed foraging patterns: the food-sharing hypothesis

Hypotheses about how hominids behaved are peculiarly hard to test. Chimpanzees and bonobos are known to share food with relatives. In the 1970s and 1980s a hominid **food-sharing hypothesis** was advanced by Glynn Isaac, who argued that early humans may have gathered food to a central point for its processing and consumption. He made extensive studies of sites where early tools and animal bones were found together. He argued that food sharing at a semi-permanent home-base would make sense if there was a **division of labour** between the sexes in food gathering. This scenario envisages males operating in bands together at a greater radius from the home-base than the females. The females, encumbered perhaps by young, would be operating more locally to the home-base in a plant-food-gathering role. What these bipedal hominids were able to carry home in their freed hands may have taken on a special social significance. If these earliest hominids had infants with long periods of childhood, a home-base (even if only temporary) might have been essential. The food-sharing hypothesis is an attractive scenario as the starting point of human cultural evolution, but there is too little evidence to confirm it as yet. Lewis Binford, an American archaeologist, subsequently criticised Glynn Isaac on this score, and Isaac had to re-evaluate the limited evidence that the earliest archaeological and bone sites provide. Nevertheless, there is evidence that early *Homo* butchered carcasses at living sites. These are littered with tools and bones. As to what happened in these places much must be left to our imagination.

9.5   Extended childhood

Early in primate evolution a reproductive strategy evolved in which single young were carried by their mother in an arboreal environment. This early selective pressure favoured a greater investment in the foetus of maternal energy and nutrients, enabling a larger-brained child to be born. Brain cells are peculiar in very largely completing their tissue development in foetal life. Brainy infants may therefore become brainy adults, but only if the infant brain with its increased storage capacity develops by the processes of learning. **Play**, an activity embracing in essence all the adult activities of feeding, fighting and social and sexual interaction, equips the young individual for society. The more fully prepared the young are, the stronger the society will be. Once the childhood period is extended, however, children remain children for longer and mothers cannot easily care for more than one at a time. But offspring that are weaned may continue learning and growing while away from mother within the wider adoptive social group. Here arboreal life limits the process as it is harder for the vulnerable young to be kept together. For the earliest hominids this would undoubtedly have been easier with a ground-level home-base served by a more co-operative food-sharing society. Only in the most social and caring milieu is **childhood extension** practicable. Its development then becomes self-fuelling, because the well-cared-for individual generates the more caring society. As effective social support of the young increases, so their improved rate of survival reduces the species' requirement for a rapid reproductive rate (see figure 9.4).

Giving birth to a **larger-brained infant** through a pelvis modified for bipedalism presents problems. Chimps have a large and backward-facing birth canal, but the *A. afarensis* female 'Lucy' had a bipedally adapted pelvis

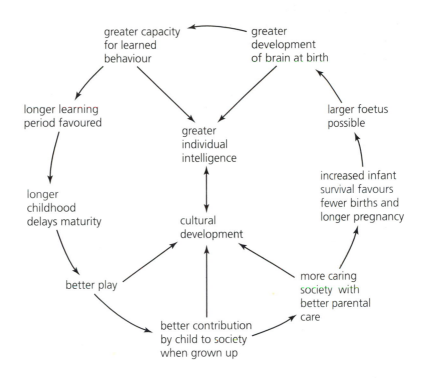

Figure 9.4 A positive feedback cycle showing the importance of extended childhood in the intellectual and cultural development of humans

in which the birth canal is relatively constricted – even considering that Lucy's infants would only have had a chimp-sized brain! Little is known of pelvises of early *Homo*, but that of a male *Homo erectus* 2 million years younger than Lucy is still very much smaller than that of modern man. There seems therefore to have been a very real cost here in human evolution: birth is more difficult for all hominids when compared to apes and the more so if the brains of their infants are to be bigger. Our human birth pattern is recently evolved. In apparent adaptation to its big head the modern human infant, just before birth, rotates in the birth passage. The soft, only partially ossified plates around its brain overlap, allowing the head to be squeezed through the pelvic aperture.

9.6   Changed sexuality

Female apes have a monthly cycle in which sexual receptivity to mating by males only occurs around the time of ovulation. The chimpanzee female, for example, exhibits swollen genitalia and reddened skin around the vaginal opening for two to five days. During this oestrous period, by her scent and coloration, she attracts the promiscuous males and although weak 'honeymoon' bondings occur with single male individuals for a few days, such liaison is generally all over after a week and any sexual approaches by males will then be resisted. That early hominids had menstrual cycles of a human kind is unlikely, for the human female cycle is physiologically unique amongst primates. There is no 'heat' or oestrous period, only a monthly 'period' for renewal of the endometrium of the uterus. Secondly, in modern human societies, pair-bonding for a long time is the general rule. What caused this sexual transformation?

Perhaps the most plausible view of the evolution of a **long-lasting pair-bond** relates to the settled home-base and the sexual division of labour envisaged in the food-sharing hypothesis. Social harmony is not favoured when there is a division of labour between males and females such that they are segregated by day, and when single females within the group become so attractive for only a short time. The males would not go away to gather food if individual females were 'on heat', as in a troop of chimpanzees or baboons. If on the other hand the receptive period of any given female is lengthened and the sexual signals of receptivity are reduced, the problem is eased. If at the same time the selection of partners is based on a broader mate preference than sex drives alone, the social system may evolve in favour of more long-lasting sexual liaisons. We can envisage males soliciting females with gathered gifts and females soliciting males with more permanent sexual signals. This then might make that crucial bond, cemented by sexual activity, whose survival advantage is the extended care of the bonded couple for their offspring. Families, however, are not self-sufficient and such a stabilised society of more or less bonded individuals would have greater survival advantage under natural selection if their family altruism extended to the whole group.

9.7   Bigger and better brains

Hominisation is thus a highly complex weaving together of food sharing, division of labour, new manual skills, speech and culture, prolonged childhood and the development of pair-bonded families and cohesive bands. It cannot all have happened at once, but imperceptibly slowly. Judging from our knowledge of other primates, much of this hominisation may predate the origins of the genus *Homo*. But there is, however, a positive feedback or self-fuelling drive to the processes described in this chapter. It is not just a question of bigger brains (see figure 9.5), but better ones. From about 3 million years ago, brains not only increased in cranial volume, but also in the outer brain cortical tissue area or **grey matter** concerned with brain control. In the chimpanzee 25% of the surface grey matter is infolded,

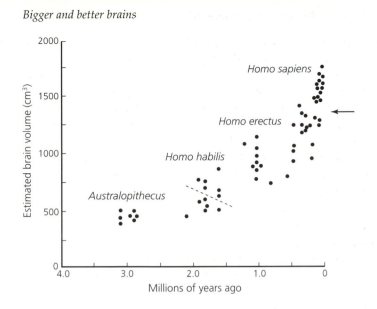

Figure 9.5 During human evolution the brain has increased in size, both absolutely and with respect to the body, especially during the past 2 million years when the stature of early humans has hardly changed. The arrow indicates modern mean value.

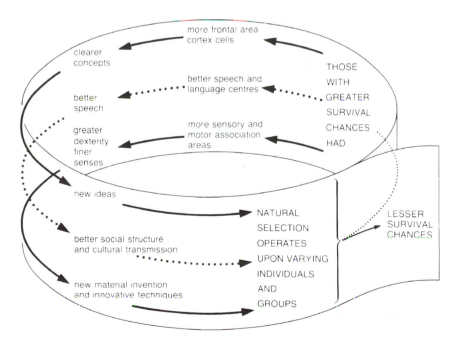

Figure 9.6 A theoretical scheme of positive feedback favouring evolution of a more complex brain

Figure 9.7 KNM-ER 1813 (left) and 1470 (right), two hominid skulls commonly assigned to *Homo habilis*, both from Koobi Fora, Kenya. ER 1470 is the more ancient, with a larger brain and a larger flatter face. ER 1813, although small-brained, is actually more 'human' in several characteristics, such as its relatively small teeth.

but in *H. sapiens* 65% is infolded to give an increased neurological control much greater than the volume change (from 400 to 1400 cm³) implies. We would expect a larger human to have a brain greater in size than that of an ape, but even when scaled for increase in size, much of the brain is at least moderately enlarged, the motor and sensory cortex is effectively doubled and the prefrontal area is some three times as large. Figure 9.6 attempts to show how natural selection acting upon individuals and groups, with necessarily genetically varied degrees of brain complexity, might lead, by survival of the fittest, to further expansion and a greater intricacy of function.

9.8 The fossil evidence for *Homo habilis*

The fossil evidence of early members of the genus *Homo* is scanty and really quite varied, posing the question of whether there was one hominising line, two or even more. The *Homo habilis* type specimen OH 7, described in 1969, comes from the lowest Bed I of the Olduvai series. Until recently this was the bed from which the earliest stone tools were known. The Olduvai fossils consist of a very human jaw, albeit narrowed and fine, and some fragments of the parietal bones indicating a brain volume of 650 cm³. Hand bones, probably of the same individual, are virtually modern though differing as described earlier in this chapter. The discovery of an earlier and much larger fossil skull at Koobi Fora in 1972 established *H. habilis* more firmly. This was the celebrated ER 1470 (see figure 9.7) discovered by Bernard Ngeneo and carefully reconstructed by Richard Leakey's team (this hominid is sometimes classified as *H. rudolfensis*). This fossil is dated at about 1.9 Ma. The cranial volume of 800 cm^3 is over 1.5 times that which would be expected in a comparably sized ape. The rest of the facial features are similar to those of the australopithecines but the jaw was less massive though equally prognathous. Contemporary finds like ER 1813 (from Koobi Fora; see figure 9.7) and OH 62 (from Olduvai) are smaller-brained and the latter shows some affinities to *Australopithecus afarensis*. The very earliest remains with *Homo* features are from Hadar in Ethiopia. In 1994 William Kimbel found an upper jaw in two fragments with a date of 2.3 Ma. This is contemporary with the earliest chipped pebble tools. Although clearly so varied in size, with a mosaic of advanced and primitive characters in these specimens, it presently seems sensible to lump them as one species – *Homo habilis*.

In summary, the diagnostic features that distinguish *Homo habilis* are increased brain size (range 500–850 cm^3) over *Australopithecus* levels (300–500 cm^3), the possession of modern hand and foot bones, no great increase in cheek teeth molarisation or decrease in incisor size, but narrower and less massive jaws than the contemporary robust forms. With its lighter jaw and larger brain, *Homo habilis* would have been more recognisably human than the portrait of Lucy. *Homo habilis* evidence spans a period from just over 2 Ma to about 1.6 Ma. So far fossils of this species only come from Eastern Africa, whereas the sucessor species *Homo erectus* is found throughout the Old World of Europe, Asia and Africa. This chapter on hominisation and evidence for *Homo habilis* has given extensive coverage to the **hypothesis making** that needs to be part of scientific investigation if steps in evolution are to be proven to have occurred. The process is highly subjective, but if the hypothesis is plausible and simple and the evidence fits the hypothesis, the plausibility increases. Such is the nature of our 'certainty' about these events.

Questions to think about

1 What is the difference between speech and language?

2 Argue either *for* or *against* the hypothesis of a division of labour between the sexes among early hominids.

3 Why might the teeth of *Homo habilis* have become much reduced in size?

TEN

Homo erectus: *tools, hunting and fire*

10.1 The Java ape-man

In the late nineteenth century **Eugene Dubois**, a young Dutchman stimulated by the implications for human ancestry implicit in Darwin's theory, determined to find the hypothetical 'pithecanthropus', half ape (pithecus) and half man (anthropus), that would constitute the missing link in Darwin's theory. He decided to look in a forested region of the tropics where apes were still found wild and where glaciations, as in Europe, had not eroded away the deep sediments in which these remains might be found. Unable to afford the cost of mounting his own expedition to Java, he joined the Dutch colonial army and in 1891, having been given charge of a group of prisoners

Figure 10.1 *Homo erectus,* a reconstruction

who he turned to fossil excavating, he found what he had always longed to find, his ape-man, **Pithecanthropus**. The few teeth, skull cap and femur bone from the banked sediments of the Solo river, at a place called **Trinil**, are the type specimen of *Pithecanthropus erectus*. The skull was so thick and low brow-ridged that ape affinities were suspected, but the brain volume, 850 cm^3, was relatively large and the femur was that of an upright, erect, hominid. Here was the ape-man that popular image sought and as such it was announced to the world by a jubilant Dubois.

The characteristically thick, low-domed skulls of *Homo erectus* have been found in Africa, Europe and Asia, dating from 1.8 to 0.2 Ma. They might span 80 000 generations over these 1.6 million years of prehistory. As there are no *Homo* fossils outside Africa with undisputed dates before 1.6 Ma it is assumed that a late *H. habilis* or early *H. erectus* achieved this migration in the early **Pleistocene**. Within Africa there may have been other branches of the human tree over this period before one anagenetic line perhaps led to the archaic form of our own species, *Homo sapiens*. Taxonomically these early humans are now lumped together in the genus *Homo*. Some would keep the name *Pithecanthropus* for the perhaps later and isolated Asian forms.

10.2 Fossil sites

Although *Homo erectus* was first recorded from Java, in Indonesia, the fossils with the earliest undisputed dates are from East Africa. In the Upper Bed II at **Olduvai** and at **Koobi Fora**, at a concordant date of 1.6 Ma, good *Homo erectus* fossils are found. The appearance of this species is also accompanied by stone tools of a new and different type. These Acheulian hand-axes are described later in this chapter. All the East African fossils with *H. erectus* features fall within a period from 1.8 Ma to the relatively recent date of 0.2 Ma, just 200 000 years ago. The most complete and early skull specimen is ER 3733 from Koobi Fora. Some taxonomists want to call this early form *Homo ergaster*. Another recent and very early find in East Africa is the **Turkana boy** (KNM-WT 15 000; see figure 10.3). Further north in Africa, later *H. erectus* fossils are found in Ethiopia, Chad, Algeria and Morocco.

Perhaps the habilines evolved into the pithecanthropines over a wide area. Outside Africa there are early *H. erectus* remains in Israel (Ubeidiya), Georgia (Dmanisi), China (Lantian) and Java (Sangiran) all with dates more than 1 million years ago. The oldest is in China at **Lantian** (possibly 1.3 Ma) where the skulls are small-brained. The **Djetis** beds at **Sangiran** have revealed what appears to be a more massive-toothed early hominid remarkably like *H. habilis* (OH 13). Although Java is an island today it would have been part of the Asian mainland in the early Pleistocene.

There are many more Asian *H. erectus* sites with more recent dates. The original Trinil **Java man** is now dated at 0.7 Ma. The remains of **Peking man** (0.5 Ma), from **Zhoukoudian** (Chou K'ou Tien) near Beijing (Peking), were

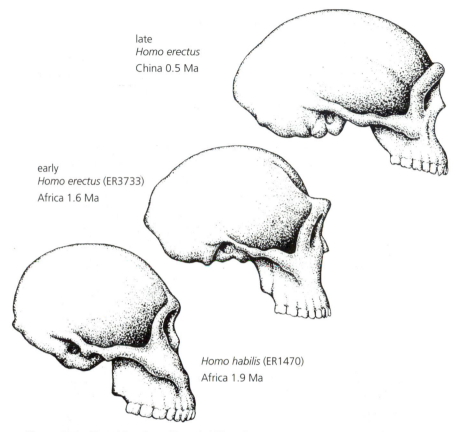

late
Homo erectus
China 0.5 Ma

early
Homo erectus (ER3733)
Africa 1.6 Ma

Homo habilis (ER1470)
Africa 1.9 Ma

Figure 10.2   Transition from *Homo habilis* to *Homo erectus*

first described in 1927. Excavation was superbly done by Franz Weidenreich and Chinese colleagues but many of the remains were lost in the 1939–45 war, leaving only plaster casts. In this collection there were a dozen skulls, several mandibles, 150 teeth and many post-cranial bones. Peking man's tool technology was primitive. They may have domesticated fire, though the evidence for this is currently disputed. They certainly lived in a seasonally cold climate and had somehow come to grips with the rigours of the first Günz glaciation 0.4 million years ago. Fossils from **Jingnuishan** (0.2 Ma) are transitional to archaic *H. sapiens*.

The European *Homo erectus* fossils, such as the Mauer mandible (Heidelberg jaw) from Germany (dated 0.35 Ma), are very rudimentary but clearly belonged to successful late members of the lineage that hunted in early Ice-Age Europe. They cannot have found these northern latitudes easy but the living sites revealed by archaeologists at **Torralba** (0.4 Ma) and **Ambrona**, in northern Spain, and at **Terra Amata**, near Nice in France, testify to their successful hunting in a European climate colder than that of today. The **Petralona** skull from Greece at 0.5 Ma has a larger brain and less protuberant brow showing affinities with archaic *Homo sapiens*.

10.3 The characteristics of *Homo erectus*

The oldest and most complete skeleton of a single early human is the **Turkana boy** (KNM-WT 15 000). This was found beside the Nariokotome River in West Turkana, Kenya, in 1984 and has been exhaustively described by Alan Walker. It is reliably dated, from overlying and underlying volcanics, at 1.6 Ma. The virtually complete skeleton of this still-growing

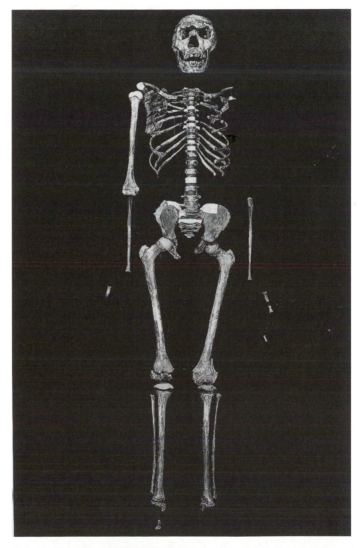

Figure 10.3 Turkana boy (KNM-WT 15 000) found at Nariokotome, Kenya in 1984. This skeleton of a young *Homo erectus* boy (less than 12 years old) is the most complete specimen of an archaic human ever discovered. It shows a tall and well-built physique, even in this young individual, and has been dated to around 1.6 million years ago.

teenager, standing 1.6 m tall, is distinguished by its slender build, full bipedality, narrow hips, small cranium (volume 900 cm^3) and a low-crowned skull. What is perhaps extraordinary is that a million years later the mean brain volume of this species was still not much greater, witness to a period of equilibrium rather than phyletic gradualism in this part of our human story (see section 6.2). The Turkana boy probably grew up faster than a modern boy, and although he might only have been 12 years old he was skeletally the equivalent of a 17-year-old (he still had no wisdom teeth).

Homo erectus was skeletally fully modern, somewhat bigger than *H. habilis*, standing from 5 to 6 feet tall (1.5–1.8 m). The skeletal bone is different, and the outer cortex is thicker in all the skeletal remains. This **robustness** would be expected if the transition from *habilis* to *erectus* was to be achieved by an allometric increase in body size. While some of the African skeletal remains indicate fully modern height, there is no doubt that Peking man was short and strong with a chunky muscular build and reduced surface area to body mass ratio. This would have aided body-heat retention in a cold temperate climate. However, it is the skull of *erectus* that is so different from our own. The **cranium** was much flattened on top, the crown running forward into a shelving down forehead which rose up and forwards into massive brow-ridges above the eyes. Viewed from above, the head was anterio-posteriorly elongated. The teeth and jaws were more massive than our own, yet the face was flatter and the jaw chinless. The **brow-ridges** buttressed and strengthened the face and provided support for large chewing muscles at the sides of the skull. Although the head was held fully upright, the foramen magnum was not quite as far under the cranium's centre of gravity as ours. To stop the head from hanging forward, massive neck muscle insertions are apparent on the back of the *H. erectus* skull. Cranial volumes of early Java specimens are in the *H. habilis* range of 600–800 cm^3, but late *H. erectus* volumes were as much as 1250 cm^3. This enlargement must partly reflect an allometric increase in stature, but the mean of the species, 880 cm^3, reflects only a very slow increase in volume and complexity over time.

10.4 Cultural evolution

Although there is little physical change in hominid form between 1.6 and 0.4 Ma, *Homo erectus* might represent a steady change in becoming mentally, socially and culturally more human. If we were able to go back a million years, we should probably find early humans in bands of about 30 individuals, feeding largely on gathered plant materials brought to a home-base or going out in tight-knit bands to scavenge meat from the kills of large carnivores and perhaps to hunt large prey for the first time. **Tools** would have been made from chosen local stones, from well-known localities, and some means of carrying water, perhaps in skins or ostrich shells, would undoubtedly have been devised, making longer journeys to another needed resource possible. Spoken language would have been rudimentary, yet it would have been a major cohesive force used to establish order in the community, to convey information and to express ideas. Children would have slowly absorbed their culture by receiving instructions, by learning for themselves and by imitating others in the social group.

At first sight these cultural features, such as a language, seem closely interwoven with a biological reality, like a language centre in the brain, but a clear distinction must be made between these two. **Cultural evolution** is fundamentally different in kind from biological evolutionary change. **Culture** is a store of information and behaviour patterns, transmitted, not by genetic inheritance, but by learning, imitation, instruction or example. Culture is not a solely human realm. The great apes have transmitted culture of a simple kind, but what began with humans as a largely biological evolutionary story ends as a predominantly cultural one. Possibly cultural features are what made *Homo erectus* a more successful species than contemporary robust australopithecines. The capacity to acquire that culture successfully and transmit it depends upon genetically inherited abilities. *Homo erectus* was probably much less gifted in this than ourselves. Biological fitness for cultural transmission may have limited their cultural evolution.

10.5 Stone tools

The making of stone tools marks the beginning of a cultural stage in evolution that leads by steps over 2 million years to our modern industrial technology. Chimpanzees today are known to be **tool-users**, and to some extent **tool-makers**, selecting and shaping sticks for termite 'fishing'. They may even arrange stones to prop up and improve on the angle of an anvil used with a hammer stone to crack a nut. However, it takes a lot of human teaching to get apes to make flake-tools. From the time of early *Homo* the physical ability to make tools improved, with all that this implies for brain–hand–eye co-ordination and control, cognitive perception of the tool and of the task to be performed. This was a biological evolutionary change. But so too improved the imitated design of tools, the choice of materials for making them, the methods of their manufacture and the diverse uses to which they were put. This was a parallel cultural change.

Oldowan culture

Perhaps as early as 2.3 Ma *Homo habilis rudolphensis* purposefully modified **pebble tools** for food preparation. The very earliest stone tools are barely recognisable as such, but where a sediment lake bed deposit contains concentrations of cobble-sized stones in a manner unlikely to have occurred by water-borne action, the suspicions of the archaeologist are aroused. The

Oldowan culture takes its name from Olduvai. Any stone-tool culture with artefacts made up predominantly of cobble-sized stones from which a few flakes have been struck off, by blows with a hammer stone, to give a hand-held **Oldowan chopper**, is characteristic. The early Oldowan tool-kit is composed of choppers and hammer stones, often of igneous basalt rock. The chipped-off percussion flakes might have been used for cutting or as scrapers. This culture was developed by *Homo habilis* and was clearly taken to Asia by the earliest *habilis/erectus* forms, for it is found at its most developed in the culture of Peking man (0.5 Ma).

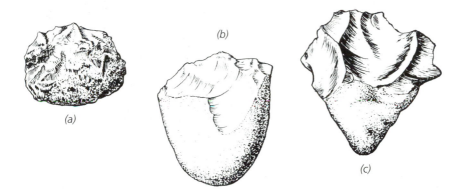

Figure 10.4 Tools of the Oldowan culture: (a) quartz spheroid from Olduvai Gorge, Tanzania; (b) basalt pebble tool, Oldowan chopper, from Olduvai; (c) flint chopping tool from Clacton-on-Sea, Essex.

Acheulian culture

The Acheulian culture, the Lower Palaeolithic hand-axe tradition, is first found at 1.6 Ma in East Africa and in Israel. It is found throughout Africa, Europe and some of Asia for more than a million years. The culture is named after Saint-Acheul, near Amiens in France, where it reached its peak 0.2 Ma ago. In Africa the earliest hand-axes appear together with *Homo erectus* fossils at 1.6 Ma at both Olduvai and Koobi Fora. The **Acheulian hand-axe** is not unlike the shape of an open flat hand (see figure 10.5). Made with the symmetry and the same size and thickness of a hand, this tool may have had some 'third hand' symbolism. With their two flat sides and two cutting edges that lead to a point, these bifaces are more difficult to make than an Oldowan chopper. When held in the hand along one edge and around the rounded end, the other edge may be used as a chopping or slicing blade. The Acheulian tool-kit also comprised stone choppers, chisels, scrapers, cleavers, awls, anvils and hammer stones. In South East Asia the minor tool-kit is found but never the large hand-axes, suggesting perhaps the use of other large tool-making materials of a less durable kind such as bamboo.

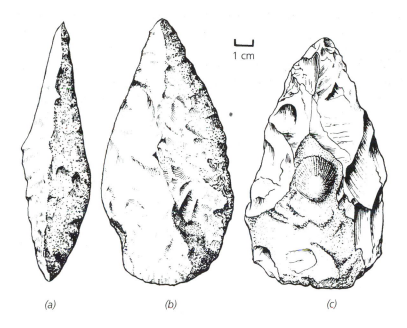

(a)   (b)   (c)

Figure 10.5 Acheulian hand-axes: (a) early Acheulian phonolite hand-axe, made by *Homo erectus*, from Olduvai Bed II, edge profile view, (b) face view; (c) late Acheulian flint hand-axe, made by *Homo sapiens* and incorporating a fossil shell in its design, from West Tofts, Norfolk.

Experimental archaeology

Stone tools and their use raise many questions about cultural evolution, some of which can be answered by an experimental approach to archaeology in which hypotheses are tested against each other with respect to the evidence gleaned from sites, where tools and fossil bones may together litter the floor of presumed living sites or home-bases. **Glynn Isaac** undertook pioneer studies at Koobi Fora sites that are over 1.5 million years old. He wished to be sure that his living-site interpretations were not over-subjective, given that these sites are 100 times older than Britain's Stone Age! He collected and mapped not only tools, but also every stone flake and fossil bone fragment he could find, and meticulously attempted to reassemble them. This laborious exercise resulted in the reconstruction of some complete stones so that the sequence in which flakes were struck off could be determined and the places on the site where this was done demonstrated. This study and the study of percussion fractures of antelope bones proved objectively and beyond doubt that these assemblages of stones and bones were indeed butchering sites and were not produced by random geological events. Another experimental archaeologist, **Peter Jones**, took more than two months to learn how to make hand-axes with ease and accuracy from materials local to Olduvai. The basalt and phonolite material was tough, and large swinging follow-through blows were needed to chip off the secondary trimming flakes that give the tool its edge. In butchering goats, Jones found that the small flakes were only any use in making skin incisions, being hard to hold and blunting easily, but the hand-axe with its weight and fair edge could skin, joint and gut almost like a knife. His hand-axes took five minutes to make, and the primary cutting edge of the sharper phonolite tools could be retouched with lighter flaking blows if it became blunt. Such studies of the materials used by early humans for making tools show how selective and how perceptive of the nature of the materials they were.

Scanning electron microscopy studies of cut fossil bones and ancient tool cutting surfaces may be made. These surfaces may be compared with modern bones cut with freshly made stone tools; the **microwear** of the cutting edge, ancient and modern, is consistent with the use of these ancient edges as butchering tools.

10.6 Scavenging, hunting and gathering scenarios

It is now thought that the litter of crunched and broken animal bones that were found by **Raymond Dart** in association with *Australopithecus africanus*, at **Makapansgat**, were in fact leopard kills. The relatively defenceless gracile australopithecine was part of the carnage. However, Dart built on his interpretations the hypothesis that these early hominids began hunting game animals. In the absence of any stone tools associated with this species, this now seems improbable, but the hypothesis that **hunting** was a cultural spur to human evolution is interesting. We know that chimpanzees are facultative carnivores, for they will occasionally catch small animals, especially the young of baboons or antelopes. This behaviour is only very occasional. We must regard some meat eating as a probability early in human evolution. The extra protein food value of game meat may have been critically important in early *Homo* diets for adequate foetal and infant brain development.

Scavenging from the kills of large carnivores is the most likely entrée to large game hunting. Driving off lions and hyenas from their kills could be achieved by group co-operation. Kills can be spotted at a distance of miles by watching the movement of vultures. There is little evidence for scavenging. Pathological changes in an *H. erectus* skeleton from Koobi Fora (KNM-ER 1808) are consistent with hypervitaminosis A that might have resulted from a hominid eating an excess of animal livers, perhaps the easiest flesh to tear from a carcass. But if driving lions off their kills was the start, true hunting of large animals is unlikely to have got underway without the level of technology seen in *Homo erectus*. Relative to the effort applied in pursuit of small game, **group co-operation** in the hunting of large herbivores would bring greater rewards in supplies of meat. The approximate number and

Table 10.1 Game animals available as a food resource to a hominid band. For a three-mile radius home range (73.23 km²), at a biomass of 250 kg ha⁻¹, this represents 1830 tonnes live weight or 915 tonnes butchered.

Ungulate species	Approximate number of individuals
Buffalo	910
Hippopotamus	590
Elephant	125
Antelopes	955
Total	2580

Source: based on Bourliere, F., 'Density and biomass of some ungulate populations in Eastern Zaire and Rwanda', *Zoologica Africana* **12** (1964), Cape Town

density of herbivorous game mammals inhabiting an area of African savannah is known from present-day National Parks. Assuming that a group of hominids with a three-mile radius home range lived in this environment, the numbers of animals in their range and their standing crop biomass may be calculated. Taking the data in table 10.1, an annual cropping of only 1% of such a resource would supply each of 50 hominids with half a kilogram of meat every day, a very generous ration.

Of the later evidences for **human hunting** skill the site at Torralba, in Spain, is the most impressive. Here, at a date of 0.4 Ma, a steep-sided valley and marshy gully was used as a funnel trap for large game driven into it by bands of people using fire. On one small site the remains of 30 elephants, 25 horses, 25 deer, 10 wild cattle and 6 rhinoceros have been found, together with cleavers, hand-axes and a litter of tool flakes. This must represent a permanent and regularly used butchery trap. Arguably hunting may have been important to the hominisation process in that it places a high premium on co-operation between individuals and would thus reinforce social organisation. The travelling and carrying would have put a strong selective pressure on **effective bipedalism**. Catching and killing requires intelligence, ingenuity and technological skills. This has positive feedback to reinforce brain development and cultural sophistication. Speech would become an increasingly important part of planning and executing a hunt.

This view of the formative nature of hunting to the life of the pithecanthropines has received a good deal of criticism from those who have studied the lives of both apes and contemporary hunter-gatherers. This is not only a **feminist viewpoint**. There is no good reason, given the vegetable diet of apes, to suppose that *Homo erectus* was more carnivorous than ourselves. Probably the hunting hypothesis is too male-centred and too romantic a scenario for practical everyday living. Females may well have hunted with men and groups of males may well have spent much more time in **gathering** activities. Tool making and use for gathering (e.g. basket making) might well be more sophisticated than for butchering, and the social and environmental skills, including the **cultural transmission** of natural history knowledge involved in a life of gathering, were probably much more formative than anything that happened in a short hunt. Daily gathered fruits and seeds are likely to have been nutritionally more important than occasional meat in the diet. At Zhoukoudian, the Beijing cave-people evidently ate deer but also, judging from seed remains, huge amounts of gathered wild fruits and berries.

10.7 Nakedness

There are innumerable theories to account for human hairlessness or **nakedness**. Probably no single theory is correct, but the sweat cooling theory, the aquatic ancestry theory and the sexual selection theory have the greatest plausibility. Tropical early hominids would have been sparsely haired and dark skinned, to be adapted to the heat and intense solar radiation. Modern apes and humans actually have equal numbers of hairs but human hair on the body is extremely fine and short. Hunting would have involved periods of intense exertion and great metabolic heat production. Only with an efficient **cooling** system could temperature regulation be achieved. Humans have several million sweat glands, at densities up to 500 per cm^2 of skin. Body sweat secretion, at rates of up to 1.6 litres per hour, can, in dry air, produce evaporative cooling effects of 3.6 MJ per hour. Whereas there is evidence for hunting behaviour there is as yet no hard evidence of an **aquatic ancestry** stage. This hypothesis, developed in a popular account by Elaine Morgan in 1972, relates not only to reduction of body hair but also to many other hominid features of interest and such ideas should be cautiously entertained. Desmond Morris in 1968 made a good case for **sexual selection** being involved in hair loss: this is a subjective but nonetheless very real consideration for modern humans, for whom the physical attributes of skin and hair (so played on by cosmetics manufacturers) play a significant part in mate selection by females and males. Few people would deny that they are influenced by such epigamic (sexual signal) characteristics in sexual attraction.

10.8 Fire

Fire has been a natural feature of tropical savannah grasslands for sufficiently long for many plant and animal forms to be adapted to it. Both volcanic events and lightning strikes can cause fires and these may burn extensively in dry seasons. Early humans undoubtedly increased the frequency of fires in such environments, since open grassland favours the highest carrying capacity of herbivorous game animals. The earliest **fire hearths** are hard to pin-point. There is a charred lake-site at Chesowinga near Lake Turkana, dated at 1.4Ma. Here the ground clay had been baked by a fire. Certainly by 0.4 Ma there was fire in use in the hunting shelters of southern France, and it was used at Torralba at 0.4 Ma for driving herds of game into a gully. Peking man may have used fire at a similar date, although this is disputed. Not only would fire have been used for warmth and frightening prey, but also for that peculiarly human activity, cooking. **Edmund Leach**, the social anthropologist, argued in 1976 that **cooking** was not just a biological necessity, destroying pathogens and softening food, but became a symbolic act or ritual which transformed the food into something clean and safe and different from its former nature. Thus fire became a tool, but one of special cultural significance. *Focus*, the Latin word for the fireplace, still retains its meaning of centrality in our language. The bright, warm, beast-defying fire became the social centre that drew together our ancestors in the dark wild nights of prehistory.

Questions to think about

1 How did the Turkana boy, from 1.6 Ma, differ from a modern human teenager?

2 What genetic inheritance is required to make a cultural inheritance possible?

3 Why do we have so much hair on our heads and so little anywhere else?

ELEVEN

Homo sapiens: *the Neanderthals and the African Eve*

11.1 The beginning of our own species

Modern hunter-gatherers such as Australian aborigines, Amazon Indians and the San Bushmen of the Kalahari are the last practitioners of a way of life once universally followed. This is the life style to which we ourselves are biologically adapted. *Homo erectus* was a hunter-gatherer a million years ago and so too were our *Homo sapiens* ancestors as recently as 15 000 years ago. In the transition there is both evolutionary biological change and huge cultural change, the two processes running side by side and interrelating continuously with each other. The evolution of the one species into the other seems a relatively short step in biological evolution but anthropologists are not at all agreed as to how it happened. We shall explore the **multi-regional hypothesis** (see section 11.2) and the **replacement** or **'out of Africa' hypothesis** (section 11.5). For a million years *Homo erectus* seemed to change little, but enormous cultural changes have overtaken *Homo sapiens* in the past 200 000 years. By their very nature these seem to impel the rate of change at an ever-increasing pace. Many of the social and technological foundations of human society were initiated in this late stone-age period.

11.2 The multi-regional hypothesis

We have seen that *Homo erectus* spread throughout the Old World, but how did *Homo sapiens* arise over the same area? Did one species give rise everywhere to the other? In 1908 Otto Schoetensack discovered a robust but clearly early human jaw at **Mauer**, near Heidelberg, in Germany. In 1959 a fossil skull was unearthed in Greece, at **Petralona**, and dated at 0.5 Ma, which is markedly unlike the heavy-browed *Homo erectus* of Asia. Both foreshadow the early *Homo sapiens* skulls known from **Steinheim**, in Germany, and from **Swanscombe**, in Kent, which date from 0.3 Ma (or 300 ka; ka means 'thousands of years'). These are clearly early *Homo sapiens* types. When compared to *Homo erectus*, the Petralona skull has a large brain volume of 1200 cm^3, a slightly higher vaulted skull, reduced brow-ridges, reduced bone thickness and smaller teeth of a less robust kind. By contrast Swanscombe and Steinheim skulls are even more recent but would still, to

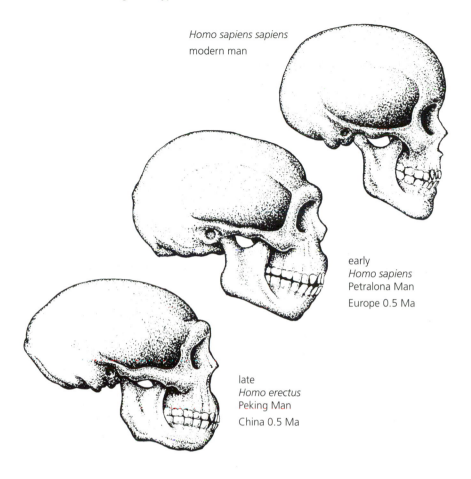

Homo sapiens sapiens
modern man

early
Homo sapiens
Petralona Man
Europe 0.5 Ma

late
Homo erectus
Peking Man
China 0.5 Ma

Figure 11.1　Transition from *Homo erectus* to *Homo sapiens sapiens*

us, be facially primitive, with heavy jaws, thick necks and long skulls. We now see these early Europeans as ancient relatives of our own species. If a race of our species, they would be referred to collectively as ***Homo sapiens heidelbergensis***. At 30 ka we find a fully modern form of human in Europe, the **Cro-Magnon** people (*Homo sapiens sapiens*). It is tempting to see this progression as a clear example of a **phyletic gradualism**, whereby the biological process of hominisation (becoming more like a modern human) is proceeding at a slow and gradual pace within one ongoing population. If we look to Africa there are remarkably late *Homo erectus* forms, as well as some large-brained but primitive-looking skulls such as that from **Kabwe** (Broken Hill) in Zambia, which dates from only 150 ka. If we look at Asia there is also a similar set of gradual changes apparent in skulls from the *H. erectus* of **Zhoukoudian** to archaic *sapiens* at **Jingniushan** and **Dali**, and again there is a transition from late *H. erectus* at **Ngandong** (Solo) in Java to early modern forms in South East Asia and Australia. This broad picture of change gave rise in the 1970s and 1980s to a clear multi-regional assumption that *Homo sapiens* had arisen across the world in all these areas, with perhaps gene-flow linking one group to another and so conserving the genetic integrity of the one species. This theory fitted in with contemporary racial ideas and the idea of five ancient **human races** (Bushmen, Negroids, Caucasians, Mongoloids and Australoids). This 'candelabra' model (see figure 11.2) of a polytypic species was to be overthrown by a reappraisal of the appearance and disappearance of the Neanderthal people and by the investigation of the antiquity of our own species, employing genetic evidence from mitochondrial DNA and the application of population genetics.

11.3 *Homo sapiens* from the ice ages

Europe and Asia have experienced quite drastic climatic changes over the past million years as the ice sheets have expanded and retreated with each of the **glaciations**. Not only did these climatic events scour the surface of the land, but at each advance they also often obliterated the early traces of humans. Only in caves and in certain lake beds and alluvial deposits have fossil bones been found. Because these are often only single specimens the picture is fragmentary, though tools and very durable artefacts may be preserved. Many of the remains of wood, fibre and skin have rotted away, a fact that may bias interpretation. The Lower Palaeolithic came to an end with the late Acheulian cultures reaching their peak just before the onset of the **Riss glaciations**. What became of the earliest *Homo sapiens* (Heidelberg) types we do not know, but they do show some affinity with the specialised Neanderthal race. A human molar and child's jaw fragment discovered at Pontnewydd cave in Wales, dated at 250 ka, show primitive Neanderthal features.

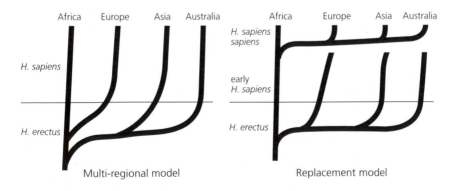

Figure 11.2   Models for multi-regional and replacement theories

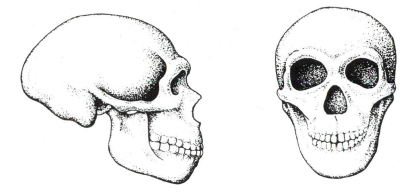

Figure 11.3   Neanderthal man, *Homo sapiens neanderthalensis*

The **Neanderthals** have for a long time fascinated students of prehistory. Their distinctive stone culture appears for the first time in Europe after the long fossil gap of the Riss glaciations at 75 ka. They developed a sophistication in stone working that gave them cultural dominance in Europe until after the close of the Second **Würm glaciation** at 25 ka. Not only was their culture new but their physical form was different, an undoubted adaptation to the rigours of survival in such cold times. For this latter reason they are regarded as a subspecies or even a full species in their own right.

11.4 The Neanderthals, *Homo sapiens neanderthalensis*

The valley of the **Neander River** (Neanderthal) is near Düsseldorf in Germany. Here in 1856 some remains were found in a limestone cave, which initially excited only local curiosity. Between 1866 and 1910 many more European cave sites revealed the remains of primitive humans. The Neanderthals gained a popular image of being more primitive than we see them today. Often, in early works, they are portrayed as hunched and stooping with massively robust and hairy limbs – the classical cartoon caveman. This image was largely due to a failure to interpret correctly one particular skeleton as being that of an elderly arthritic man; they were as upright and as un-apelike as we are. The classic Neanderthal from the early Würm glaciation was stocky, powerfully muscular with large joints and hands. They had strangely enlarged pelves, perhaps to make the birth of large-brained infants easier. Possibly females were pregnant for a full year and gave birth to much bigger, less helpless infants. The skulls were distinctive, being long and low-domed like those of *Homo erectus*, but only moderately brow-ridged and of much larger cranial volume (see figure 11.3). So far as brain size is concerned, their mean volume was greater than that of modern humans, a fact which may reflect the need to control more musculature than we possess. The jaws were robust with a molar gap between the last molar, the wisdom tooth and the ascending branch of the jaw bone. They may well have had a higher larynx than ourselves with less capacity for speech but, on the credit side, less likelihood of choking. They had a ridged occipital protruberance at the back of the skull with a larger nuchal area for neck muscle attachment below it. One feature of interest is the much enlarged nasal cavity; Neanderthals are often portrayed with broad and bulbous noses. Such a physiological adaptation, in their cold climate, would have conserved both heat and moisture in the freezing air. It is worth noting that the cold-adapted elk (moose), saiga antelope and reindeer, all hunted by Neanderthals, have relatively large nasal cavities too.

We have more archaeological evidence on the Neanderthal way of life than for any previous type of human. Controversy rages continuously as to how we should interpret their artefacts and considerable remains (see Further reading: Neanderthal titles by Trinkaus and Shipman, 1993, and Stringer and Gamble, 1993). That they had a greater level of human consciousness is shown by the fact that they were the first people to ritually bury their dead, indicating some awareness of the personal significance of death. Some Neanderthals were buried with the skulls of large carnivores arranged, presumably symbolically, around the corpse. Neanderthals apparently made no ornaments for themselves and seemed not to use bone and antler tools as later Upper Palaeolithic people did. At burial sites such as those at Le Moustier in France, there are abundant evidences of what is thereby named the **Mousterian flake culture**. Flake cultures differ from the Acheulian hand-axe culture in that bladed flakes are struck from a core, whereas an Acheulian hand-axe is the core stone from which flakes were struck. In Eurasia, the Mousterian culture was a refinement by the Neanderthals of an earlier **Levallois** flake culture, which began 300 000 years ago in Africa. In the Mousterian technology, only the finest flaking glass-like silicate minerals such as flint and obsidian were used and these were finely retouched to give a more effective edge. A large tabular block of flint was first obtained and struck with a single heavy blow to produce a conical core. From this core, flakes were struck by single heavy blows to give very fine tools with razor-sharp edges. Retouching, a finer flaking of the cutting edge, was done by lighter percussion from a more elastic hammer such as a long bone or piece of hard wood. Mousterian retouched flakes, such as side-scrapers, notches, points and denticulates, would have been used for such things as skinning, sharpening sticks, as spear points or as fine saws (see figure 11.4).

The Neanderthals were spread over much of Europe and Western Asia where the climate was like that of the present-day tundra but immensely rich in large herds of game animals. Although caves give us the best remains, it is probable that tent shelters were more commonly used as the home-base. Much detailed archaeology in the **Ukraine** has shown that these bands of hunters killed reindeer, wild horses, moose and mammoths in the northern

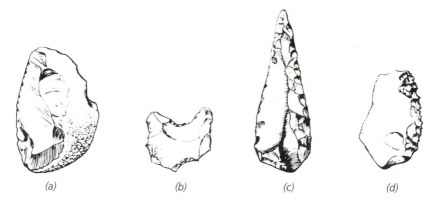

(a)   (b)   (c)   (d)

Figure 11.4   The Mousterian tool-kit of Neanderthal man: (a) sidescraper tool for skinning; (b) notch tool for stick sharpening; (c) point, spear head; (d) denticulate saw.

plains and wild sheep and deer in the south towards the Black Sea. Ukrainian sites are thought to have centred on large shelters, about nine metres wide and three metres in height, built of branches arching together and overlain with skins, and often weighted down with the bones of mammoths. Only bones, fire hearths and Mousterian flint tools remain to suggest what life was like for a hunting band of Neanderthals. Some notion of their clothing, for example, may be deduced from the initially puzzling fact that at excavated sites fox, wolf and hare skeletons are found without their foot bones. This might possibly mean that these animals were skinned with the feet left in the skin as ties for attachment. In confirmation of this plausible hypothesis no needles have been found which could have been used for sewing, but only the foot bones of those animals, grouped together inside the shelter, the skins having long since rotted away! How these people hunted and trapped so efficiently is still not known. It is presumed that cave sites such as **Les Eyzies** and **Combe Grenal**, in France, were used seasonally, as here game mammals would have migrated north and south, to and from summer and winter grazing. Sun drying, smoking or freezing of this meat could have supplied protein needs between migrations, and the gathering of fruits and other plant foods would have been possible in summer to broaden the diet.

   We do not know who brought the Mousterian tool-flaking techniques to Europe, although their earliest development seems to have been in South West Africa at the time of the Riss glaciation in Europe. Although both the skeletal form and the culture of the Neanderthals took a long time to develop, their departure from the scene is really abrupt. At the close of the Second Würm glaciation, and after 40 000 years of Neanderthal predominance, these people and their Mousterian culture seem to disappear as suddenly as the ice sheets themselves. To the south, less specialised Neanderthals were found. These are typified by the **Mount Carmel** finds, in Israel, in the cave of **Mugharet es Skuhl**, dated at 40 ka. It is generally supposed that less cold-adapted forms of *Homo sapiens*, or more modern forms from Africa, moved north and west into Europe, for at 35 ka fully modern *Homo sapiens sapiens* remains are found. The last Neanderthals lingered on until about 25 ka in Spain.

Why did the Neanderthals disappear? Three reasons are commonly advanced. First, their technology, though an improvement on the Acheulian, was far inferior to the stone working and skill displayed by **Upper Palaeolithic** people. Secondly, their heavy build and probably demanding nutritional requirements were not an advantage in the mid-Würm inter-glacial (35 ka). Thirdly, their sociocultural level was inferior to that of their successors whose jewellery, figurines and cave paintings mark the golden age of prehistory. From a genetic viewpoint it is possible to see how these descendants of *H. s. heidelbergensis* underwent adaptive change and isolation over 50 000 years to become the Neanderthal subspecies or species. However, their skull form and skeletal features disappear from the fossil record within 5000 years, more rapidly than could have occurred by natural selection alone. All evidence now points to the changes in human physical form and culture being due to the arrival of modern humans, *Homo sapiens sapiens*, from elsewhere.

11.5 The replacement hypothesis: out of Africa again

In 1981 **mitochondrial DNA** was sequenced for the first time. Mitochondria, the respiratory powerhouses of the cell, have a circular DNA strand of 16 500 base pairs (see section 5.7). Mitochondria are maternally inherited, that is in any individual they are far more likely to come from the mother rather than the father because so little paternal cytoplasm is involved in sperm fertilisa-tion of an egg. Your mitochondria come to you from your mother, your maternal grandmother and your great-grandmother before that. In 1987 Rebecca Cann, Mark Stoneking and Allan Wilson published data on mito-chondrial DNA (mtDNA) samples collected from 150 people from all around the world. They were expecting thereby to establish clear racial groupings. Using restriction endonucleases they analysed the sequence of the bases and fed the data into a computer to work out the simplest (most parsimonious) phylogenetic relationships of these people. As a result, and contrary to expec-tation, no clear 'races' were at all obvious. Moreover, based upon the rates of mtDNA evolution in other groups of mammals in relation to the fossil record, it was clear that all these humans were extremely closely related. For example, much larger differences were found between different chimpanzee populations and between different gorilla populations. The **molecular clock** evidence seemed to indicate a very recent point of origin for all these modern people, at around 200 ka. This conclusion has attracted a popular image perhaps more inflated than either its biological or statistical significance deserve. It is often referred to as the **African Eve hypothesis**.

Biologically, because we have genes from both our parents, from four grandparents and from eight great-grandparents, we are clearly each descended from a huge variety of individuals. Yet if you look only at the mtDNA (the genetic usefulness of which is relatively trivial) it will be apparent that if a large group of people trace back far enough down only one line (the female one), they are likely eventually all to share the same ancestor. This is to say, 'Eve' is no more important as an ancestor than any other single one of her relatives around at the time. Because we find the earliest modern *Homo sapiens sapiens* fossils in Africa (at 125 ka), it makes it doubly probable that the '**African Eve**' existed earlier, somewhere in Africa, at around 200 ka. This was before modern humans moved out of the continent to supplant the archaic humans that had already colonised Eurasia in preceding emigrations. There are no fossils yet known of modern humans outside Africa before 100 ka. In support of this hypothesis, there is a greater degree of mtDNA variation in Africa than in the indigenous populations of the remainder of the world.

In 1997 Matthias Krings, Mark Stoneking and a research team in Munich, Germany made an analysis of some much-fragmented mtDNA from the right humerus of the original Neanderthal type specimen. Using PCR (polymerase chain reaction) techniques on a 328 base-pair region of mtDNA, it was shown that the average difference in coding among a large sample of modern humans is only about 8 base pairs, that between humans and chimps is about 55 base pairs, and that between this single Neanderthal and the range of modern humans is about 27 base pairs. Careful controls were done. This places the separation of the Neanderthal line from the modern human line at well over half a million years ago. Despite their brain sizes (which placed them as '*sapiens*'), many palaeoanthropologists will now argue for the removal of both the Heidelbergs and the later Neanderthals from *Homo sapiens* into their own species, *Homo heidelbergensis* and *Homo neanderthalensis* respectively. This use of PCR DNA technology opens up the possibility of similar investigations of other recent fossil humans.

Where does all this leave the multi-regional hypothesis? It is not entirely disproven, since this evidence only involves mitochondrial DNA. Was there a reproductive barrier between these recent human species? How could we now tell? Some supporters of the multi-regional model are still sceptical of what might be seen as flimsy genetic evidence.

11.6 The final evolution of *Homo sapiens sapiens*

What were the biological skeletal changes that led to the evolution of our own species in Africa? Principally there was a thinning and lightening of bones, a greater development of the vaulted cranium and steep forehead, reduced skull length and a further reduction of the jaws. As the teeth were bunched up closer in the jaw and drawn back under the face, a more prominent chin developed. The gap between the last molar and the ascending jaw branch closes and there is a definite tendency, still continuing today, for the last molars not to erupt, or to do so with too little room for comfort. This shift of physical character to a more lightly built juvenile form can be seen as an example of **heterochrony**, a shift in developmental pace (see section 6.3). **Neoteny** is the retention, in evolution, of some more characteristically juvenile feature in the adult form of a species. It is a common evolutionary development displayed by many groups of animals, and as long ago as 1920 Louis Bolk suggested that this process of prolongation of juvenile features was centrally responsible for much of human evolutionary transformation from the apes. Today the argument for neoteny goes as follows: if certain juvenile characteristics are selectively favoured, their retention into adult life may occur by the genes that produce such features being reinforced or prolonged in their expression; at the same time, if the genes responsible for the more adult thick-boned skull and skeleton are less favoured by selection, such robust characteristics might diminish. Growth patterns are known to be governed by sets of genes and gene switches, turning the developmental system on and off. This in turn affects patterns and rates of growth, the latter often being mediated by hormones. Two pertinent examples of hormone-mediated changes will illustrate this. Melatonin, a hormone from the pineal gland, influences the onset of puberty, while somatotrophin, the growth hormone, stimulates the growth of bone. The evolution of a large-brained, small-jawed *H. sapiens sapiens* with reduced body hair, light skeleton and late puberty can all be argued to be neotenous developments in our species evolution, achieved by relatively minor genetic change.

Cooking and tool developments would certainly reduce selection for powerful jaws while tool-use might reduce selection for massive individual strength. Perhaps sexual selection for more juvenile facial features, like the high forehead and small jaw, could have contributed to change.

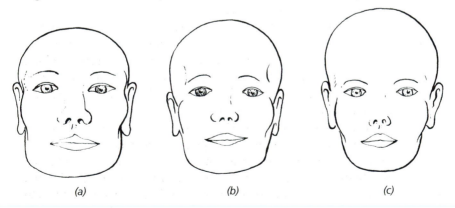

(a) (b) (c)

Figure 11.5 Neotenisation of the human face. From left to right: jaw size decreases, cranial height increases at the expense of cranial length, relative nose size decreases. Based on (a) a Neanderthal skull; (b) a Cro-Magnon skull; (c) a more juvenile face showing these trends.

Figure 11.6 The Bull of Lascaux. Once hunted by Palaeolithic humans, the fierce auroch (*Bos primigenius*) was domesticated in later Neolithic times. Wild cattle were hunted to extinction in historic times.

11.7 Cro-Magnon people and the Upper Palaeolithic culture

This final stage of human biological evolution is represented by many fossils from caves with Upper Palaeolithic artefacts. The type specimen is **Cro-Magnon man**, dated at about 30 ka, and coming from the Dordogne region of France. Taller and finer boned than the preceding Neanderthals, these people were skeletally little different from ourselves. While the human skeleton has changed little in the past 30 000 years, the same cannot be said for human culture which has changed dramatically.

The last European cave-men had a very sophisticated culture, as witnessed by their impressive cave art at places such as **Lascaux** in France and **Altamira** in Spain. Nobody seeing these art forms can fail to be moved by their sensitivity, skill of execution and imaginative display. Ritual burial sites reveal the development of jewellery; coloured beads and pierced teeth were strung together or stitched to skins and ivory bracelets were worn. Upper Palaeolithic tools are characterised by the very long flakes struck from a cylindrical core. This was done by indirect percussion, with an antler-tine punch which was rested on the edge of the core block and then struck by a hammer blow, or by using a heavy chest pressure flaking staff with a pointed end (see figure 11.8).

The manufacture of more blades in less time and from less flint made this technology highly efficient. A kilogram flint core could be worked to

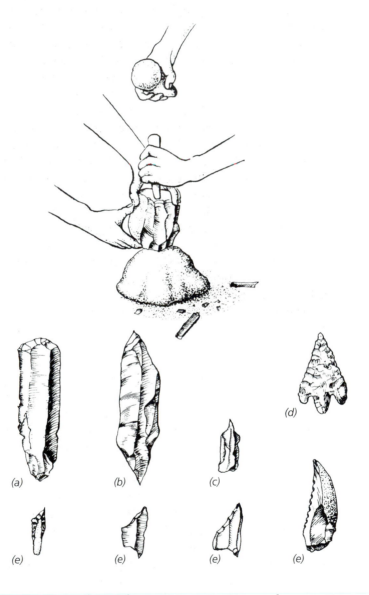

Figure 11.7 The Upper Palaeolithic tool-kit of Cro-Magnon humans. Using a hammer stone and antler-tine punch, long-bladed flakes were struck from a flint core placed on a stone anvil. Flakes were then retouched to make such things as (a) an end scraper, (b) a burin chisel, (c) a microburin drill, and (e) microliths (barbs).

yield 50 good blades with a total cutting-edge length of 25 m. These long flakes were then retouched to make knives, saws and pointed chisel burins. Tiny flint points and barbs, the so-called microliths, were also developed. These could be fitted to arrows and harpoons. Different tool-kits for different functions, such as fishing, are found. The first use of the bow and arrow is hard to date, but it was certainly used in hunting in Upper Palaeolithic times. The survival of these people in the Third and Fourth Würm glaciations was even more impressive than that of their Neanderthal predecessors. This survival was possible because of their superior tool-kits and technology, now using bone, antler and ivory as well as flint as the tool materials. The bow-drill, derived from the hunting bow, made it possible to make holes to thread beads and to drill bone needle eyes for stitching skins. For the first time there is also evidence of basketry. Baskets must have made fruit and nut gathering much easier, as well as providing better storage for gathered food. Until the domestication of fire, all human energy was derived from human muscle power alone, though solar power as heat, for example for drying, had its uses. Extrasomatic energy sources clearly gave humans an increased capacity to exploit their environment. Fire was undoubtedly the first of these, providing heat, sterilisation of cooked food, extension of the day length, hardening of sticks and heat tempering of flints or the driving of game. The smoking of meat and laying-up of gathered food stores for winter gave humans extrasomatic food reserves. Animal furs aided heat conservation. An even more sophisticated form of increased efficiency in energy and material harvesting was the exploitation of game migration routes. This effectively meant that the biological productivity of a much larger area could be tapped at one point, thus reducing the energy expenditure that would be involved in collecting from the game animals' entire range.

In Europe, at the close of the Würm glaciation era just 15 000 years ago, there lived fully modern people of sophisticated yet still stone-age culture. Similar human evolutionary development occurred elsewhere. During the early Würm glaciation the ice caps were so great that the world's sea-levels fell markedly. This made the water barrier between continents and islands less formidable, and Australia was colonised 35 000 years ago from South East Asia. This date also marks the extinction of the Australian Megafauna. Australian aboriginal fossil ancestors are known at Mungo, dated at 30 ka. Probably successive waves of Upper Palaeolithic peoples invaded the Australian continent, crossing the deep Torres Strait by canoe. The early Mongoloids, whose Upper Palaeolithic culture mirrors that of Europe, crossed the frozen Bering Straits into Arctic North America as recently as 12 000 years ago to people the whole of pre-Columbian America, from Greenland down to Tierra del Fuego. Here again the continent's giant mammals became extinct. In South Africa, the skulls from Fishoek, at 30 ka, are very like modern Bushmen and Hottentots. Since the last interglacial 35 000 years ago, modern humans have been one diverse single subspecies, *Homo sapiens sapiens*. As culture picked up and passed on ideas, the human species' power over its environment suddenly increased beyond the normal energy and physical limits for a hominid, so setting the scene for the dawn of agriculture and the earliest civilisations.

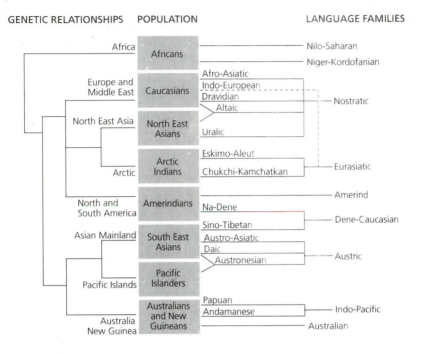

Figure 11.8   Genetic relationships and language families

11.8 Race and culture

Today we see ourselves as one species. The genetic differences within any one ethnic group are vastly greater than the differences between groups. Genetically we are **polymorphic** rather than truly **polytypic**. The physical differences between modern peoples are attributable to the different climatic and environmental adaptations and the different cultural concepts of hand-someness and beauty that we have, and upon which natural selection and sexual selection respectively have operated. These external physical differences disguise our internal similarities. In 1991, a leading human geneticist, Luigi Cavalli-Sforza, investigated the distribution of 127 alleles in blood samples from 42 different human populations. The concordance between these data and our notion of modern human expansion is astonishing (see figure 11.6). On this cladogram the genetic distance between the African populations and the rest is greatest (or longest ago in terms of time for change). The Australian groups separated next with the South East Asian groups. The northern Mongoloids gave rise to the Amerindians. The Western Asians (Caucasians) gave rise to the Europeans.

We know that language is entirely culturally based. Intriguingly, these genetic affinities tie up concordantly with the recent evolution of our **languages**. A century ago, Jacob Grimm, the collector of fairy tales, researched the evolution of European languages. Most of the languages of Europe he traced back to an Indo-European tongue that had its probable origin before the Neolithic revolution 12 000 years ago (see chapter 12).

Questions to think about

1 What are the differences between the multi-regional hypothesis and the replacement or 'out of Africa' hypothesis for the evolution of modern humans?

2 Are we over-dismissive of the Neanderthal people? In what ways were they successful?

3 Do some research in a library with books on archaeology. How many of your home utensils, household, garden or workshop tools had a stone-age equivalent?

TWELVE

The Neolithic revolution: the end of prehistory

12.1 How farming began

About 15 000 years ago, that is around 13 000 BC, the last Würm glaciation came slowly to an end. During the glaciation, ice sheets had covered up to a quarter of the Earth's surface and the deposited ice lay thousands of metres thick, as it still does in Greenland. The long thaw, which continued for several millennia, brought not only a rise in temperature but also higher sea-levels. Warmer seas led to greater evaporation and increased rainfall. In Eurasia the plants and animals adapted to the temperate zone, which had once been forced south by the ice age, moved north again; cold arid tundras gave way to warm moist woodlands. The hunted herbivores such as reindeer and elk moved north to be replaced from the south by various species of deer and wild cattle in the lowlands and wild sheep and goats in the hills. The retreat of the ice allowed a freer movement of isolated animals and plants. Certainly, for humans, freed migrations may have resulted in an enrichment of genetic diversity. In this last postglacial epoch our fully modern hunter-gatherer ancestors first settled to farming.

One of the mysteries of this pre-civilisation period is the shift by hunter-gatherers to settled farming all around the world. It is best documented in the Near East, but major areas of **animal and plant domestication** occurred elsewhere long before the historical age of exploration. Table 12.1 shows the striking parallelism of six centres of endemism (places from which our domestic plants and animals originally came).

This chapter will focus entirely on the Near East. This was one of the earliest centres of domestication and the most pertinent to Europe.

12.2 The Neolithic and Mesolithic

The term **Neolithic**, the New Stone Age, was originally defined by the artefacts discovered. In Northern Europe, such finds as developed and decorated pottery and polished flint axes came to be associated with early farming. But the Neolithic culture did not arise as soon as the ice retreated, and there was an intervening transition period before it known as the **Mesolithic** – the Middle Stone Age. The Mesolithic is loosely defined as a

Table 12.1 The centres of endemism where plants and animals were originally domesticated

Area of domestication	Animal species	Plant species
Near East	Cattle, sheep, goat, pig, dog	Barley, wheat, lentils, chickpeas
China	Dog, horse, pig, goldfish	Millet, rice
South East Asia	Water buffalo, gaur, banteng and jungle fowl (chicken)	Rice, bananas, sugar cane, citrus fruits, coconuts, taro, yams
Equatorial Africa	Guinea fowl	Millet, sorghum, dates, yams, coffee, melons
Mexico	Turkey fowl	Maize, squashes, beans, pumpkins
Andean region	Llama, guinea pig	Lima beans, sweet potatoes, cassava, groundnuts

postglacial and yet pre-agricultural period in which the hunter-gatherer communities became more settled and more diversified relative to each other. They retained the sophisticated use of microliths for spears, harpoons and sickles developed in the Upper Palaeolithic and developed more sophisticated basketry and pottery. They became less nomadic, certainly no longer living in caves for most of the year, but constructing hut shelters in the open instead. Life was probably less harsh than during the ice age and there was evidently abundant game and especially good fishing. The rise in sea-levels to cover the present continental shelf around Britain meant that waters were rich in soil nutrients, and there is evidence from oyster shell middens, some of them several metres deep, that shellfish were a major dietary item. In northern Europe, this **Maglemosian culture** is the predominant example of Mesolithic life. At **Star Carr** in Yorkshire, excellent remains have been found, at a radiocarbon date of 7500 BC, of a lakeside seasonal camp in which wooden paddles, dug-out canoes and hunting bows have been preserved together with microliths of flint and tools of bone and antler.

The Mesolithic is an ill-defined period, however, for the Near East, where Old World farming began around 9000 BC, so that the Upper Palaeolithic shades almost imperceptibly into the Neolithic. In Britain the Mesolithic continued beyond the fifth millennium BC, that is until Neolithic peoples, or their culture, introduced the practice of farming. In each area of the world the story of cultural evolution is obviously different. In the Near

East, the earliest domestication of plants and animals began very soon after the last ice age. Where this first started, in a small nuclear region, the culture has been termed **Proto-Neolithic** to distinguish it from the Mesolithic that continued elsewhere. When settled farming was developed by more and more people, the cultures of those with these successful new methods are described as typically **Neolithic**.

12.3 The nuclear region of the Near East

At the end of the nineteenth century, Alphonse de Candolle, a Swiss botanist, suggested (on the basis of no real archaeological evidence) that the origin of agriculture was in the Near East, where grasses which were clearly related to modern wheat and barley grew wild. The occurrence of wild sheep and goats in this area lent strength to his hypothesis. Although interest in the ancient civilisations of Babylon and Egypt, at the edge of this area, was intense at the end of the nineteenth century, it is only since the 1930s that evidence has been forthcoming to prove that the Near Eastern geographical area was indeed the nuclear region for the origins of agriculture in the Old World (see figure 12.1).

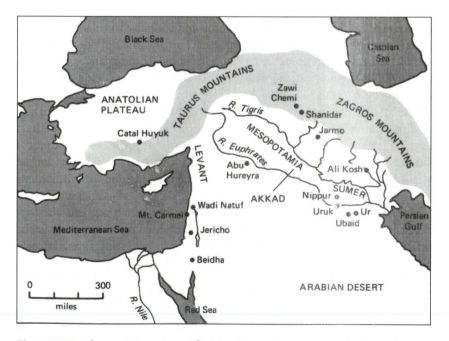

Figure 12.1 The nuclear region of the Near East, where many early domestications of animals and plants occurred and where agriculture first gave rise to civilisation.

In the eastern Mediterranean the coastal countries of Israel, Lebanon, Syria and southern Turkey form one climatic zone, the **Levant**, influenced by the Mediterranean Sea. These areas receive a regular winter rainfall and have hot dry summers. Further to the north, the **Taurus Mountains** of Turkey and, round to the southeast, the **Zagros Mountains** of Iran form a range with flanking foothills and plateaux and have a regular winter rainfall and the same hot dry summers. These uplands drain southwest into the great Tigris and Euphrates rivers which empty into the Persian Gulf, at present-day Basra, close to the ancient city of Babylon. To the south of the whole area are deserts. The present-day countries of Israel, Jordan, Syria, Lebanon, Turkey, Iraq and western Iran thus constitute a centre where many of the earliest domestications are believed to have occurred. This area of the **Nile delta**, Levant and **Mesopotamia** (literally, the 'between rivers' region bounded by the Tigris and the Euphrates) is known as the **Fertile Crescent**, being the presumed area where early agriculture and civilisation began. But today we believe that it is probably to the north of the crescent in the Taurus and Zagros range of foothills that the earliest domestications occurred. This is regarded as the very centre of events for it corresponds most closely to the habitat requirements of the first domesticated species.

12.4 The Proto-Neolithic culture of the Natufians

In a cave in the **Wadi Natuf** of Galilee, excavations in 1927 first revealed the remains of a culture that predominated in the whole of this now desert area. Between 12 800 BC and 10 500 BC, such **Natufian** sites are found at Jericho in the deepest layers of the city, on Mount Carmel, at 'Ain Mallaha in the Jordan Rift and at Abu Hureyra in Syria. The Natufians were not farmers but they had made some important first steps and can be described as **incipient agriculturists**. Firstly, these sites contain trace carbonised remains of many wild cereal seeds such as einkorn wheat and the natural tetraploid emmer wheat, as well as two-rowed barley (see section 12.8). Secondly, there are many sickles, made from deer antlers, grooved to take a series of microlith blades (see figure 12.2). The microwear sheen of these blades, studied under the scanning electron microscope, shows that they were used for cutting tough grass stems. Pestles, mortars, basalt and limestone grinding stones and stone storage bins in the ground of the hut sites indicate that the harvested cereal grains were processed and a considerable surplus stored. Jack Harlan, an agricultural archaeologist, has studied the almost pure stands of wild **einkorn** wheat that still grow in certain upland environments, the stands being almost as dense as a cultivated wheat field. By experiment he found that he could gather by hand alone 1 kg of edible grain per hour. He increased his rate by 20% using a Natufian sickle. Wild einkorn grows on rocky hills and he estimated that altitude differences would have extended the natural harvest period to at least three weeks. In this time alone

Figure 12.2   Antler sickle fitted with flint blades, used by the Natufians to harvest grain on Mount Carmel

a family could gather most of their annual carbohydrate needs without tilling, sowing or domestication changes to the wild species. Although the Natufians were fairly settled people, on account of their milling and storage technology, they also relied on fishing, hunting and mollusc-eating for animal protein. There is no evidence of any animal domestication, though herds of deer and gazelles may have been followed in hunting and perhaps protected for the first time from other predators.

Contemporary with these Natufian sedentary grain collectors of the Levant, the new occupants of the once-Neanderthal **Shanidar** cave in northern Iraq were beginning to domesticate the wild sheep of the Zagros Mountains. The Shanidar cave itself was perhaps now only used in winter, but at **Zawi Chemi**, nearby, are the remains of a classical Proto-Neolithic village dated at 9000 BC. Evidence indicates that the people depended upon gathered wheat, legumes, acorns and pistachio nuts. Wild pigs, cattle, sheep, deer and goats were all hunted, but the bones of young sheep are particularly abundant and many archaeologists interpret this as being due to selective culling from a large tended herd. Zawi Chemi has the bones of dogs which are physically distinguishable from those of a wolf. The usefulness of such domesticated dogs was probably only in hunting at first, but their presence in this situation may signify their use in herding for the first time.

12.5 Farming begins

It is important at this point to be clear about what we mean by such words and phrases as 'agriculture', 'food production' and 'domestication'. A farming system dependent upon domesticated plants and animals has four component activities:

- **propagation** a purposive breeding of animals or sowing of seeds;
- **husbandry** a care of growing animals and growing plants;
- **harvesting** the collection of the food resources that were propagated and husbanded;
- **conservation** the retention of a reservoir of selected seed and animals to breed from.

With such a system the earliest farmers must have anticipated an increased yield by their propagation, husbandry and conserving efforts, for otherwise they would have remained hunter-gatherers and just stuck to the harvesting alone. The perception of increased yields, or at least increased ease of harvesting, must also have persisted for a long time, for once functional farming began the cultivated species themselves would have altered their biological adaptations to suit the farming process to which they were subjected. The animals and plants, in other words, evolved by **artificial selection** into domesticated species. The characteristics of these domesticated species and their importance to human evolution are discussed in sections 12.7 and 12.8.

It is important to ask ourselves why these perceptions of the benefits of farming developed at all, for in the case of the Natufians and the Zawi Chemi hunter-gatherers subsistence seems to have been quite satisfactory. Anthropological studies of the San Bushmen of South Africa, present-day hunter-gatherers, show quite clearly that theirs is not a very harsh way of life and that only rarely is there great food shortage. Leisure time is apparently abundant and there are also fewer demanding daily commitments. Why should clearly successful hunter-gatherers settle down to village life and allow themselves to become tied to crops, to the risk of crop failure, to domestic animals and to the demands of their constant attention? This is a question that is at present not fully answered, but several hypotheses have been put forward, of which three are summarised below.

1   The nuclear zone hypothesis
If the hunter-gatherers and wild cereals and ruminants shared the same habitat a close living relationship of a symbiotic kind would have developed so that any 'experimental farming' would have further increased their mutual interdependence. The more settled people became, the more plants and animals they would have had to tend and the less likely they would be to move with all their farming and food processing equipment. They would have come to live in permanent villages.

2   The population pressure hypothesis
The process of adopting farming might have been intensified by demographic factors. Once food storage was adopted there would be virtually no starvation. Primitive birth controls, such as infanticide, may have lessened and the better nutrition of the population may have prolonged and increased human fertility. Population expansion would have created pressures for more efficient food production, hence more crops would be sown and tended and animals more protectively herded.

3   The marginal zone hypothesis
If the optimal environments of the nuclear zone produced the greatest population expansion, then emigration away would be inevitable if the people had lost their hunter-gatherer-adapted population controls. If the population overspilled into marginal areas, where traditional hunting and gathering

were difficult, the people would be under pressure to find food. They might thus take with them the nuclear region plants and animals so that a food supply could be ensured.

These three hypotheses are not mutually exclusive. They may be taken together to explain why the cereals and ruminants of one small area of the Near East came to be the basis of the first farming and to spread out so rapidly from their centre of origin.

12.6 Neolithic farming communities

Between 8000 and 5000 BC farming practices became much more established in the Near East and began to displace the Mesolithic cultures. Investigations of contemporary sites during this period reveal not only the variety of types of settled community, but also that hunting and gathering continued as well. The **Neolithic revolution** in food production, as envisaged by Gordon Childe who coined the phrase in 1936, was not uniform nor indeed did it probably seem revolutionary at the time. But farming must have had some edge on the old way of life, even if it was just less trouble to live in one place all the time rather than to be continually on the move. Moreover, **sedentism**, the term used for a settled village life rather than a nomadic one, favoured the development of many cultural features besides farming.

By 6750 BC at **Jarmo** in Iraq, in the original nuclear zone, there was a considerable village of 150–200 inhabitants. Goats and sheep were herded and barley and einkorn wheat were of the domesticated species form, while emmer was transitional from the wild cereal. Crude pottery containers and finely worked stone bowls have been found. Mortars and querns (stone hand-mills) were in use for food processing and the presence of polished stone axes and adzes (cutting tools) are indicative of a dependence on woodworking. Pigs, horses and wild cattle were still hunted rather than domesticated.

At **Abu Hureyra**, in Syria, a much larger settlement has been unearthed dating from 7500–5000 BC. Einkorn wheat, barley and lentils were grown and emmer wheat was later domesticated. There is evidence at this site on the edge of the Mesopotamian plain that irrigation was employed. Early in the settlement's history, gazelle, sheep and goats were herded, but by 6000 BC the gazelles had declined and cattle and pigs had entered domestication for the first time. The size of Abu Hureyra's community indicates some additional village involvement in trade. Obsidian, a volcanic glass that makes the finest microliths, was imported from Turkey along with agate and malachite stones for adornment and cosmetic use. Turquoise stones and cowry shells indicate trade with Sinai and the Red Sea coast.

At **Çatal Hüyük** in Turkey, between 6000 and 5500 BC, an even larger community had developed a town of mud-built pit dwellings, consisting of single rooms five metres square set around open courtyards. These buildings, unlike the earlier round dwellings, were roofed with beams and thatch and entered from above by a ladder. Like Abu Hureyra, Çatal Hüyük was a trade centre, and was one of the first sites where common wheat is found. It is the earliest site at which cattle were undoubtedly domesticated, the remains of many young animals being found together with biface butchering tools on the town site itself. Although such large Neolithic settlements as this may have housed several hundred people, most of the villages are not envisaged as having more than one or two hundred inhabitants at the most. For all settlements, agriculture, hunting and gathering employed almost all of the population. Trade was by reciprocal barter and the practice of crafts such as pottery and basketry was largely home-based.

12.7 Domesticated animals

The ruminant herbivores (sheep, goats, cattle) are the most important domesticated animal group for they have the capacity to digest cellulose and thus do not compete directly for the same food resources as humans. Ecologically, through domestication of ruminants, humans have therefore directed more of the available food resources in the environment towards themselves than would have been possible by hunting alone. These ruminants have a natural sociability, or **herd instinct**, in the wild. This social feature is exploited in the leading and following that herding involves (see figure 12.3). The available archaeological evidence suggests that each ruminant herbivore species that was domesticated had one centre of origin and that their first domesticators relied upon just this one herd animal species for a long period before the subsequent variety of kept animals developed. Domestication would have involved selection for particular carcass features, skin and horn characteristics and that docility and tractability without which they would have been unmanageable. It would have been the awkward or aggressive beast that went first to be slaughtered.

Sheep, *Ovis aries*, were domesticated from about 9000 BC from *Ovis ammon*, the wild sheep of the Taurus–Zagros range. Today these wild animals prefer rolling hilly country and maintain a subclimax short-grass pasture land. Domesticated sheep have largely lost their horns, or they are at least much reduced. They are shorter in stature and their mutton has a much higher muscle-fat content. Wild sheep have long hair (kemp) and short underwool. Under domestication the wool has increased and the kemp decreased to give a warmer fleece. There is no evidence of wool weaving until 4000 BC.

Goats, *Capra hircus*, are descended from the wild goats of southwest Asia. Found exclusively at some sites such as Ali Kosh, and later together

Figure 12.3 Wild goats showing the 'herd instinct' of leading and following, a trait undoubtedly exploited by humans in their domestication

with sheep and cattle at others, goats are believed to have been first domesticated in the Zagros Mountains in about 8000 BC. Although rocky mountain dwellers, under domestication they fulfilled an ecological role different from sheep, browsing from bushes and trees. Goats perhaps became more important as deforestation and the consequent environmental desiccation progressed in the Near East in the late Neolithic and early historic times, since they can subsist on very dry and marginal land.

Cattle, *Bos tauros*, were first domesticated from the wild auroch or *Bos primigenius* of the Anatolian plateau, north of the Taurus Mountains in central Turkey. Large, long-horned and extremely fierce, they must have been most difficult to domesticate, but by late Egyptian times they had become, by artificial selection, short-horned and much smaller in size. Probably first domesticated in 6500 BC, they became the most important ruminant animal in lowland Mesopotamia and Egypt where the long-grass alluvial plain pastures suited them better. Horn, thick hide, meat and milk were important products of cattle, but their unique contribution was to provide animal traction (see figure 12.5). Cattle-power released humans from tilling the land and extended the cultivable area of the early Mesopotamian civilisation.

Dogs, *Canis familiaris*, were undoubtedly domesticated by Mesolithic hunters from the small wild wolf, *Canis lupus*. This may have happened many times and in different places but the earliest Near Eastern remains date from 11 000 BC and hence this is the very earliest animal domestication that occurred. Remains of dogs are very rare at early sites in the Neolithic, so their presence cannot be assumed. The dog's role in hunting and subsequently in herding is only surmise but it might have been important in achieving the symbiosis between herd animals and man. The natural sociability of wolves enabled the early dog to respond to human society in its characteristic social way.

Pigs, *Sus sus*, were domesticated from the wild boar, *Sus scrofa*. Being a non-ruminant omnivore, its value as a domestic animal came late in the Neolithic agricultural revolution: it was hunted at first but not domesticated until 6500 BC. The omnivorous pig was useful as a scavenger on the village food surpluses, thereby returning waste to human consumption as useful meat and fat.

After the novel use of the ox, the adoption of other large mammals for transportation developed quite rapidly. The **donkey** was domesticated from the wild ass in early Egypt in 4000 BC but the **horse** and **camel** were not domesticated until after 3000 BC, in central East Asia and southern Arabia respectively.

12.8 Domesticated plants

Cereal grasses are by far the most important domesticated plants because their mature fruits, or grains, are a concentrated form of edible carbohydrate and other valuable nutrients which can be stored. Wild cereal grasses are characterised by their smaller seed grain, firmly attached glumes and bracts, with hairy awns, and a central axis (the rachis) which shatters when the grain is ripe. These adaptations cause mature seed to fall, perhaps becoming attached to a mammal's fur for dispersal and then self-seeding into the soil by means of the attached hairy awn. **Domesticated cereals** have lost the shattering rachis adaptation, enabling the whole head to be harvested without loss of grain; the bearding of awns is often reduced; the glumes and bracts more easily detach and are winnowed off as chaff; there are more florets per head and grains are larger.

Archaeological identification of seeds clearly requires close reference to wild and domesticated species. Casts of cereal grains or plant impressions are found in clay and bricks, while in certain excavated tombs, such as those in Ancient Egypt, the grains themselves remain. Experimental genetics using wild species of grasses has demonstrated beyond doubt that the tetraploid emmer and hexaploid common wheat arose as allopolyploids (self-fertilising strains arising from initially sterile hybrids by accidental chromosome doubling).

Wheat developed as follows: einkorn, *Triticum monococcum*, was first fully domesticated in the mountainous regions of the Tauros–Zagros range. This is the distribution centre of its wild precursor *T. boeoticum*, *T. monococcum* being distinguished by its larger grain and non-shattering head. This

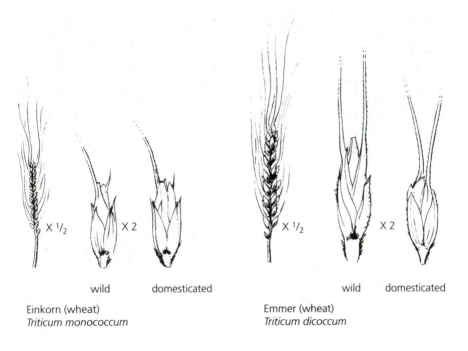

wild   domesticated   wild   domesticated

Einkorn (wheat)   Emmer (wheat)
Triticum monococcum   *Triticum dicoccum*

Figure 12.4 Ear and spikelets of early wheat. In the early domestication of wheat from wild grasses, the cultivated forms had denser and more compact heads, less tendency to shed seeds, shorter and less hairy awns, and a heavier, shorter broad grain than their wild counterparts. (After Renfrew, J., *Palaeoethnobotany*, Methuen 1973.)

latter feature, first recorded at **Ali Kosh** in 7000 BC, implies that by then the heads were harvested intact, threshed and winnowed and the seed grain later sown deliberately. Emmer, the natural tetraploid wheat, arose as an allopolyploid of einkorn and a wild grass and was gathered in its wild form *T. dicoccoides* by the Natufians in Galilee as early as 11 000 BC, but does not appear in its domesticated form, *T. dicoccum*, until 7000 BC at several sites outside its distributional centre in the Galilee region. The hexaploid *T. aestivum*, common wheat, arose during cultivation as early as 5500 BC as an allopolyploid of emmer and another wild grass; this is the floodplain-irrigated wheat upon which Mesopotamian and Egyptian civilisation thrived.

Barley was domesticated early in the Levant or in the nuclear region between 7000 and 6000 BC; there is also a transition from two-row to six-row varieties, thereby increasing yields. The species is tolerant of a wide range of climatic conditions and initially was quite as important as the wheats.

Among the **legumes**, pulses were originally simply gathered, but later they entered cultivation in the Neolithic of the Near East. Peas and lentils were derived from wild species that still grow as weeds of cereal crops. Under artificial selection, farmed lentils show a progressive increase in seed size during the Neolithic (from a mean of 2.5 mm to 6.5 mm in diameter).

Figure 12.5   Babylonian mural. Male scribes are shown recording, on wet clay tablets, transported goods and livestock (800 BC). Note the figure at the top herding goats and sheep. Oxen are shown yoked to a simple cart carrying women and children. Note also the date palm, widely grown in Mesopotamia by this period.

12.9 The beginnings of civilisation

The Neolithic, compared with the pace of all the change that preceded it, was indeed a revolution. Ecologically, humans became more closely bound with their food-source species, in ways that modified the lives of both; the first domesticated sheep and cereals could no more have survived without humans than the people could subsist without them. Hunter-gatherer ways thus became harder to return to. Hunting, once a livelihood, now became a sport. Gathering diminished, as gardens with their herbs and fruit orchards grew up around the now permanent Neolithic villages. Stored food grains in the Near East had a special importance as traded wealth, a means of exchange and, through their surpluses, a means of engaging non-farmers in other specialist artisan roles.

From 5000 BC advanced farming villages gave way to larger more populous temple-towns. Society became more complex. These communities allied to form the first political dynasties of Mesopotamia. Technologies improved, metal working began, ploughs and carts evolved. New art flourished and along with pottery came clay tablets – the biblical 'tablets of stone' – on which writing first developed (see figure 12.5). From then on a diversity of material uses, of energy exploitation and of communications increased exponentially. And when written records begin, the rest of our human evolution story is history.

Questions to think about

1 What possible thoughts might have gone through the mind of a Natufian who had just found some plants with large and nutritious seeds?

2 Describe the evolutionary scenario leading from a wild wolf to a working sheep-dog.

3 What are the advantages of herding over hunting, and what are the disadvantages?

Endpiece: what is a human being?

There are few more fundamental questions for us personally than 'What is a human being?' There is of course no single answer, but we can make concise statements of a descriptive kind on the biological characteristics of our species.

Classification

The modern human, *Homo sapiens sapiens*, is a highly polymorphic species, with many local forms showing climatic adaptations; despite this variation, there is a single gene pool. The beginning of the genus *Homo* is relatively indefinable in time, but humans in this sense are at least 2.5 million years old. The species name, *Homo sapiens*, is used to define the most recently evolved people with fully enlarged brains and sophisticated culture, making the species about half a million years old. All modern humans are of the sub-species *Homo sapiens sapiens* typified by forms prevalent for the past 35 000 years. Humans are the only surviving species in what was once a more diverse family of upright walkers, the hominids, and are now most closely related taxonomically to the living African apes, for like humans these also are hominoid, catarrhine, anthropoid primates.

Anatomy

Humans are the only living upright bipedal hominids. The legs are relatively long, having an arched and highly modified foot with an enlarged adducted big toe which is not opposable to the other toes. The pelvis is broad with expanded ilia for gluteus muscle attachment. The birth canal is small relative to the head size of infants at birth. The femurs incline from the hip towards the midline at the knee. The sinuous spinal column is held vertically, not curved forward as in apes but having characteristic retroflexions in the neck and lumbar regions. The shoulder and arm are highly mobile, especially in the young, and the hand is prehensile and finely opposable. The thorax is broad not deep. The erectly held head is almost balanced on the neck, necessitating only slight supporting neck musculature. The foramen magnum is beneath the skull. The cranial volume is approximately 1400 cm³, which when scaled for size is a brain volume to body weight ratio unequalled among primates. The cranial bones are rounded over the brain which has much enlarged frontal, temporal and parietal lobes and marked cortical folding. The face is drawn under the high forehead, there being no marked brow-ridges. There is a larger and lower larynx enabling complex vocal sound production. The teeth are much reduced for a hominid, are even in the tooth row, and arranged in a parabolic arcade. The last molars are very late to appear. The reduced lower jaw is strengthened by a protruding chin. Body hair is especially thick on the head, but elsewhere hair shafts are thin and short to the extent of apparent nakedness. There is a marked sexual dimorphism of secondary sexual characters. Sweat glands are numerous.

Growth and physiology

There is a prolonged pregnancy resulting in the birth of a large-brained yet still very underdeveloped infant. There is further delay before puberty, hence longer childhood and a longer lifespan than any other primate. Brain physiology is highly complex, the production of learned syntactic language and the degree of fine motor control of face and hands being special features. Learning and memory are prodigious and thought and self-consciousness, if not unique to humans, is unique in its extent. The skin is a very specialised and efficient thermoregulatory organ. Breeding may occur at any season and females have no oestrous period. Diet is not at all specific and feeding is omnivorous. Highly processed foods are consumed.

Behaviour

Infants are completely helpless at birth and depend upon a long period of learning and socialisation, which in fact continues through life. Gestural, facial and vocal signalling are complex, largely culturally developed and exclusively so in the case of the syntactic language in speech. Body adornment for utility, comfort, ritual or epigamic display is common (i.e. clothes, make-up, hairstyles). Males and females are strongly pair-bonded for many years, with family or kinship groups collecting into increasingly large social units. The largest societies are extremely complex and hierarchical. Social behaviour is altruistic and sharing, yet also keenly opportunistic and competitive. Communal care and communal aggression are, by animal standards, extreme. The individual's thought, reflective self-consciousness and inventive imagination find powerful social expression in the knowledge, moral order and cultural developments of society. Because behavioural adaptation is very largely cultural, humans have the behavioural plasticity to adapt to environments created by themselves.

Ecology

Humans have entered into numerous exosymbioses with plants and animals, which themselves have evolved to fulfil human habitat requirements. Much food energy is channelled through these organisms to humans in their diet. Other, non-biological energy sources are exploited, particularly fossil fuels. Living and non-living environmental materials are used and modified by technology to improve the human environment. Despite this, many environmental resources are over-exploited and the environment is polluted by technological products. Some human habitats are entirely man-made. Increasingly, competing species, disease organisms and parasites are largely controlled. Innumerable other species and their habitats are being destroyed in the expansion of this species' own preferred environment. The characteristically exponential human population growth curve shows signs of being checked by density-dependent factors such as community- imposed limits, lack of food resources and mutual community destruction. Adaptation to environment is unstable and future prospects without a modification of ecology are unsustainable.

The author is aware of the danger of treating humans in this rather cursory manner; describing the classification, anatomy, physiology, behaviour and ecology of ourselves as if we were yet one more biological species to be described. But for too long humans have seen themselves as being outside the animal world, as a creation for whom the rules were somehow different. Darwin's evolutionary theory and much recent biological science has stripped us of that privilege, for we are closely bound to our biological past and now perceive how biologically constrained we may actually be. Our society needs the depth of an evolutionary perspective and scientific world view in order to fully understand its ills. As Cyrano de Bergerac (1619–55) once remarked, we also need to address 'the intolerable pride of human beings who are convinced that Nature was made for them alone'.

Further reading

Titles marked * are recommended as good further reading for students. Those marked † are particularly good sources of illustrations. Books are listed by author's surname, initial, title, publisher and date. Articles in journals are given similarly but, following the article title and journal name, the number of the journal is given and the first page number of the article quoted. Electronic data searches in popular journals like *Scientific American, New Scientist, Nature* and *Science* will always yield the most up-to-date information.

* † Aiello, L.C. & Dean, M.C. *An introduction to human evolutionary anatomy*, Academic Press, 1990

† Attenborough, D. *Life on Earth*, Collins, 1979

* † Bilsborough, A. *Human evolution*, Blackie, 1992

Chamberlain, A. *Human remains: interpreting the past*, Trustees of the British Museum, 1994

Darwin, C.R. *Origin of Species*, John Murray, 1859

Darwin, F. (Ed.) *The Life and Letters of Charles Darwin* (3 vols, including an autobiographical chapter), John Murray, 1887

* † Day, M. *Guide to fossil man* (4th Ed.), University of Chicago Press, 1988

* Diamond, J. *The rise and fall of the third chimpanzee*, Radius, 1991

* † Foley, R.A. *Humans before humanity*, Longman, 1995

Gamble, C. *Timewalking*, Thames and Hudson, 1994

* † Goodall, J. *The chimpanzees of Gombe*, Harvard University Press, 1986

Gribbin, J. & Cherfas, J. *The monkey puzzle*, Triad/Granada, 1982

Halliday, T. *Sexual strategies*, University of Chicago Press, 1980

* † Johanson, D.C. & Edey, M. *Lucy: the beginnings of humankind*, Simon and Schuster, 1981

† Johanson, D.C. & Edgar, B. *From Lucy to language*, Weidenfeld and Nicholson, 1996

Further reading

* † Jones, S., Pilbeam, D. & Martin, R.D. (Eds.) *The Cambridge encyclopedia of human evolution*, Cambridge University Press, 1992

† Kingdon, J. *Self-made man*, Simon and Schuster, 1993

* Klein, R.G. *The human career*, University of Chicago Press, 1989

† Lanting, F. & de Waal, F. *Bonobo: the forgotten ape*, University of California Press, 1997

Leach, E. *Culture and communication*, Cambridge University Press, 1976

† Leakey, R. & Lewin, R. *Origins*, MacDonald and Janes, 1977

* † Leakey, R. & Lewin, R. *Origins reconsidered: in search of what makes us human*, Doubleday, 1992

* † Lewin, R. *Bones of contention: controversies in the search for human origins*, Simon and Schuster, 1987

* † Lewin, R. *In the age of mankind*, Smithsonian Books, 1988

* † Lewin, R. *Human evolution: an illustrated introduction* (3rd Ed.), Blackwell Scientific Publications, 1993

* Morgan, E. *The descent of woman*, Souvenir Press, 1972

* Morris, D. *The naked ape*, Jonathan Cape, 1967

Napier, J. 'The evolution of the hand', *Scientific American* **207**:308, 1964

Pinker, S. *The language instinct*, Allen Lane, 1994

* Ridley, M. *The red queen: sex and the evolution of human nature*, Viking, 1993

Ridley, M. *Evolution*, Blackwell Scientific Publications, 1993

Savage-Rumbaugh, S. & Lewin, R. *Kanzi: the ape at the brink of the human mind*, John Wiley, 1994

Shaw, T. 'Man's use of energy', *History Today*, January 1981

* † Shipman, P. *The life history of a fossil*, Harvard University Press, 1981

Shreve, J. *The Neanderthal enigma*, Viking, 1995

Slater, P.J.B. & Halliday, T.R. *Behaviour and evolution*, Cambridge University Press, 1994

* † Smith, F.H. & Spencer, F. *The Neanderthals*, Thames and Hudson, 1985

Spencer, F. *Piltdown: a scientific forgery*, BMNH/Oxford University Press, 1990

* † Stringer, C. & Gamble, C. *In search of the Neanderthals: solving the puzzle of human origins*, Thames and Hudson, 1993

Further reading

* Stringer, C. & Mackie, R. *African exodus: the origins of modern humanity*, Cape, 1996

Tanner, N. *On becoming human*, Cambridge University Press, 1981

* † Tattersall, I. *The fossil trail*, Oxford University Press, 1995

Theunissen, B. *Eugene Dubois and the ape-man from Java: the history of the first 'missing link' and its discoverer*, Kluwer Academic Publishers, 1991

* Trinkhaus, E. *The emergence of modern humans*, Cambridge University Press, 1989

* Trinkhaus, E. & Shipman, P. *The Neanderthals: changing the image of mankind*, Knopf, 1993

Walker, A. & Shipman, P. *The wisdom of bones: in search of human origins*, Weidenfeld and Nicholson, 1996

* Wilson, E.O. *Sociobiology*, Belknap/Harvard, 1976

Index